MY BIG BOOK OF MEASUREMENT

THIS BOOK BELONGS TO :

_____

_____

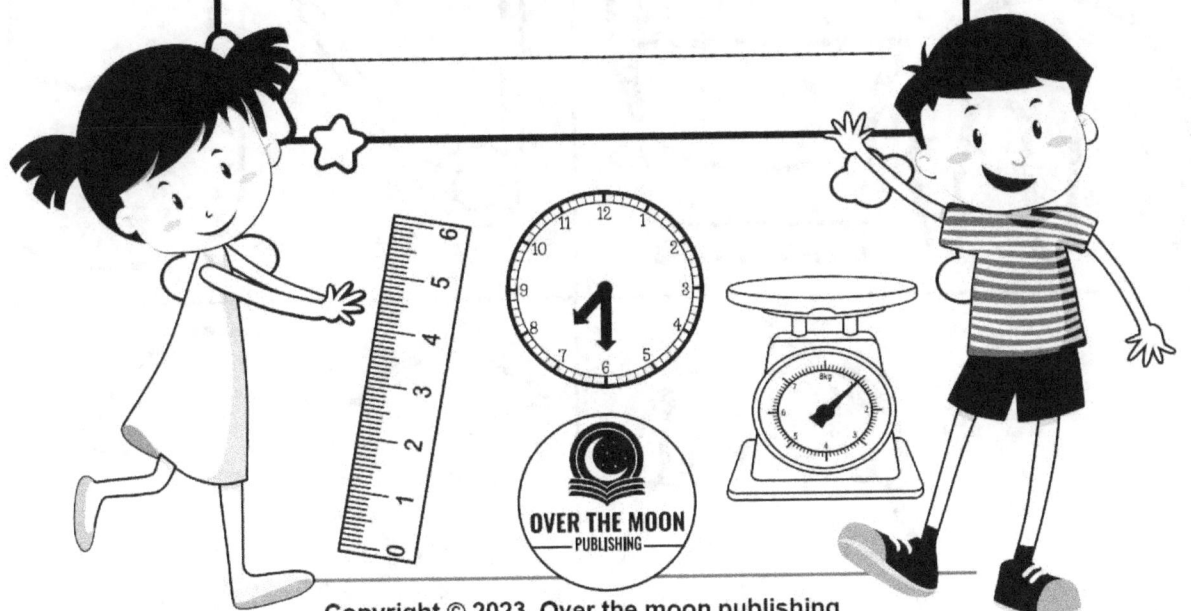

Copyright © 2023 Over the moon publishing

PLEASE NOTE - this workbook only introduces children to the concept of measuring and does not utilise actual measurements.

● ● ●

To join our mailing list and see other titles available

Website: www.captaintimpublishing.com
Email: info@captaintimpublishing.com

SHORTER AND TALLER

Directions: Color the object that is taller.

SHORTER AND TALLER

Directions: Color the object that is shorter.

MEASURING HEIGHT

Directions: For each child, count the height of the cubes and color them.

MEASURING HEIGHT

Directions: For each item, count the height of the cubes and color them.

SHORTEST TO LONGEST

Directions: Number the items in order of length from shortest to longest.

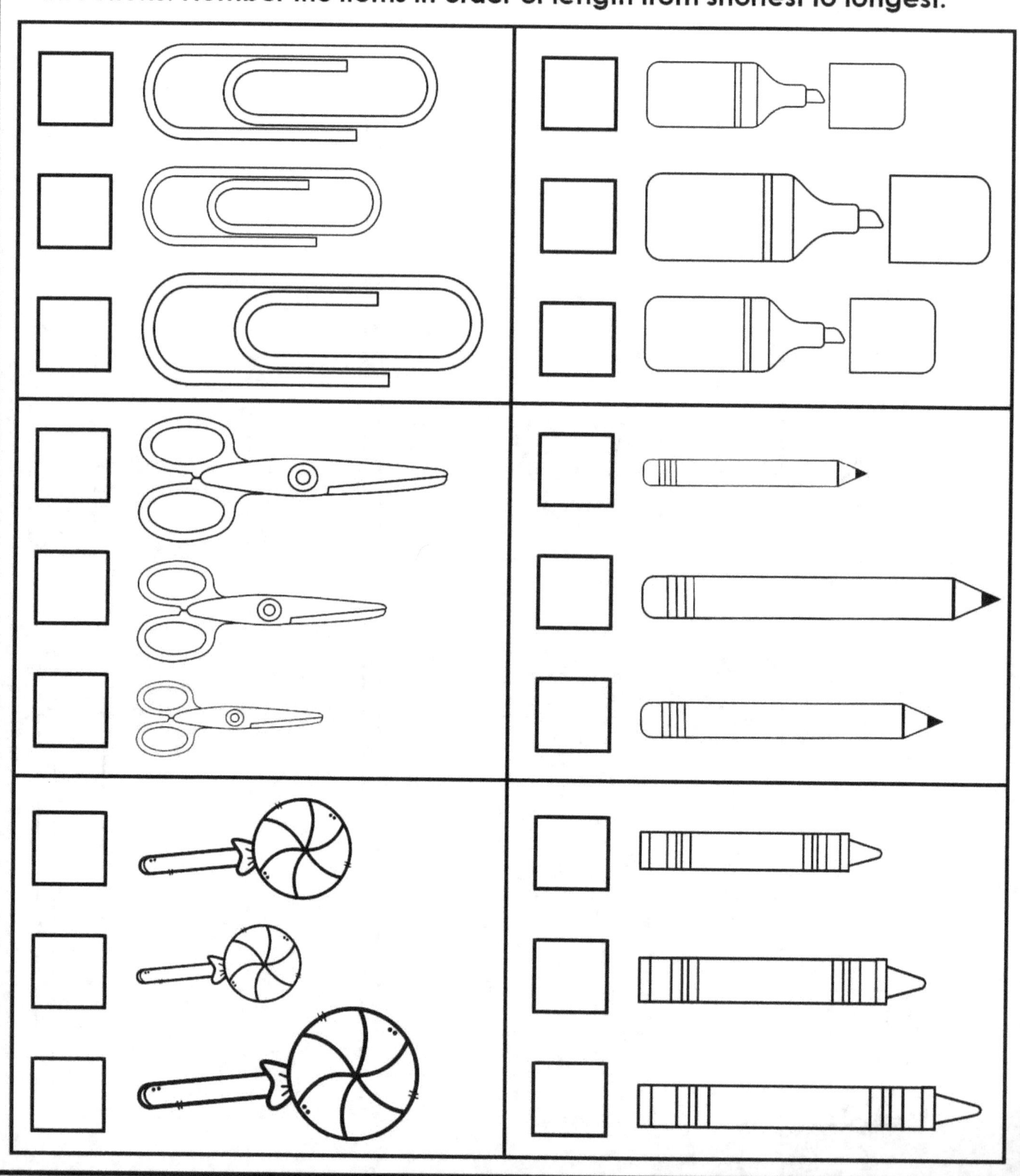

SHORTEST TO LONGEST

Directions: Number the items in order of length from shortest to longest.

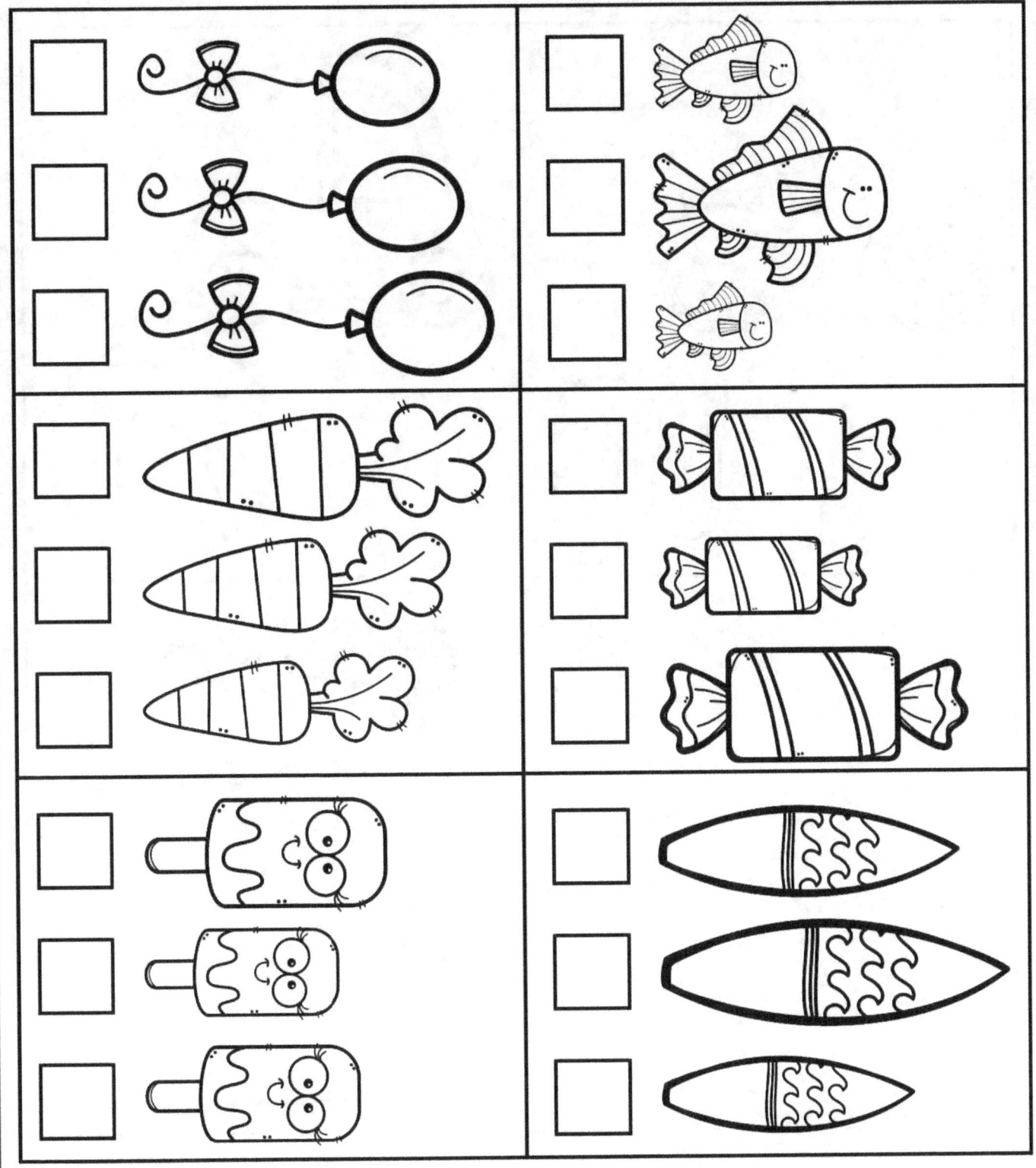

HEAVIER OR LIGHTER

Directions: Color the object that is heavier.

HEAVIER OR LIGHTER

Directions: Color the object that is lighter.

HEAVIER OR LIGHTER

Directions: Color the correct answer.

Which is lighter?

Cactus Pot	Flower Pot	Same

Which is heavier?

Orange	Same	Banana

Which is heavier?

Cookie Jar	Eraser	Same

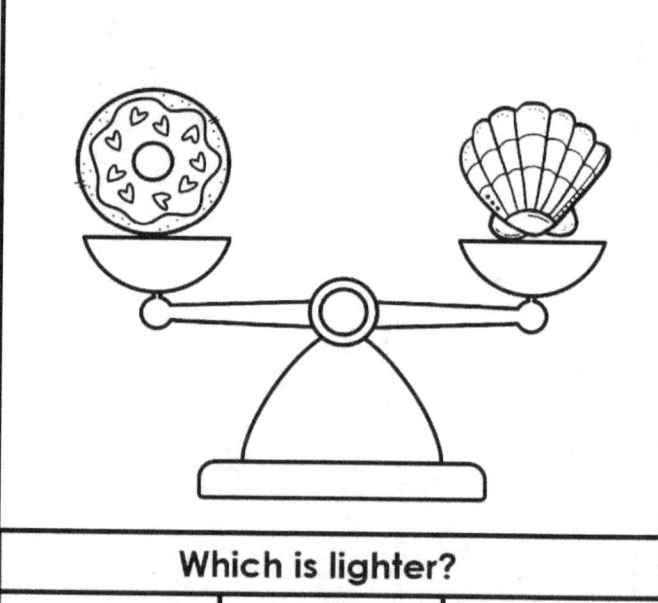

Which is lighter?

Donut	Shell	Same

HEAVIER OR LIGHTER

Directions: Color the correct answer.

Which is heavier?

Highlighter	Earth	Same

Which is lighter?

Car	Toy	Same

Which is heavier?

Same	Snail	Sunglasses

Which is lighter?

Volleyball	Party Hat	Same

MEASURING LENGTH

Directions: Color the ruler to the correct centimeters.

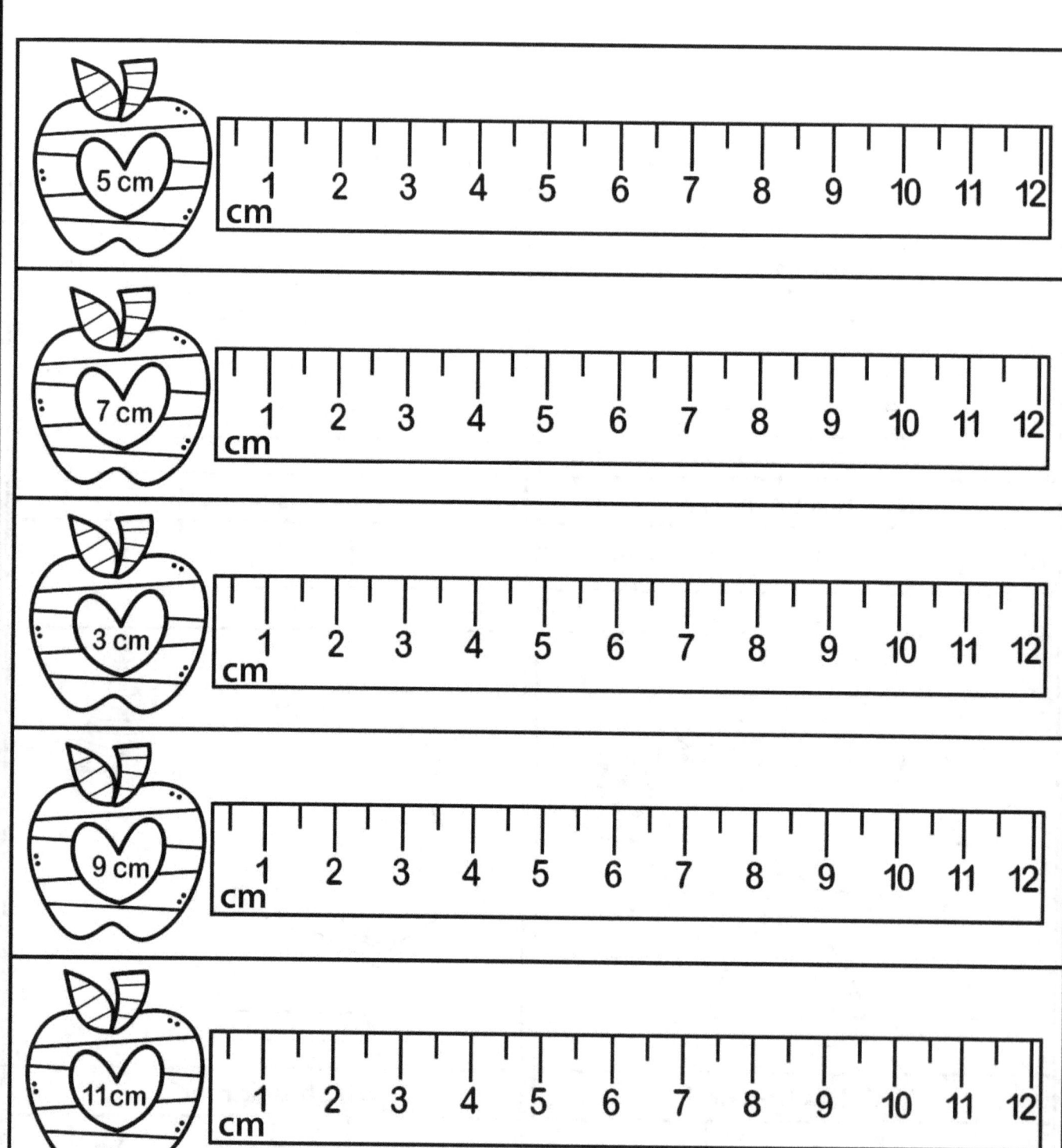

MEASURING LENGTH

Directions: Color the ruler to show how long the items are, and write your answer in the box.

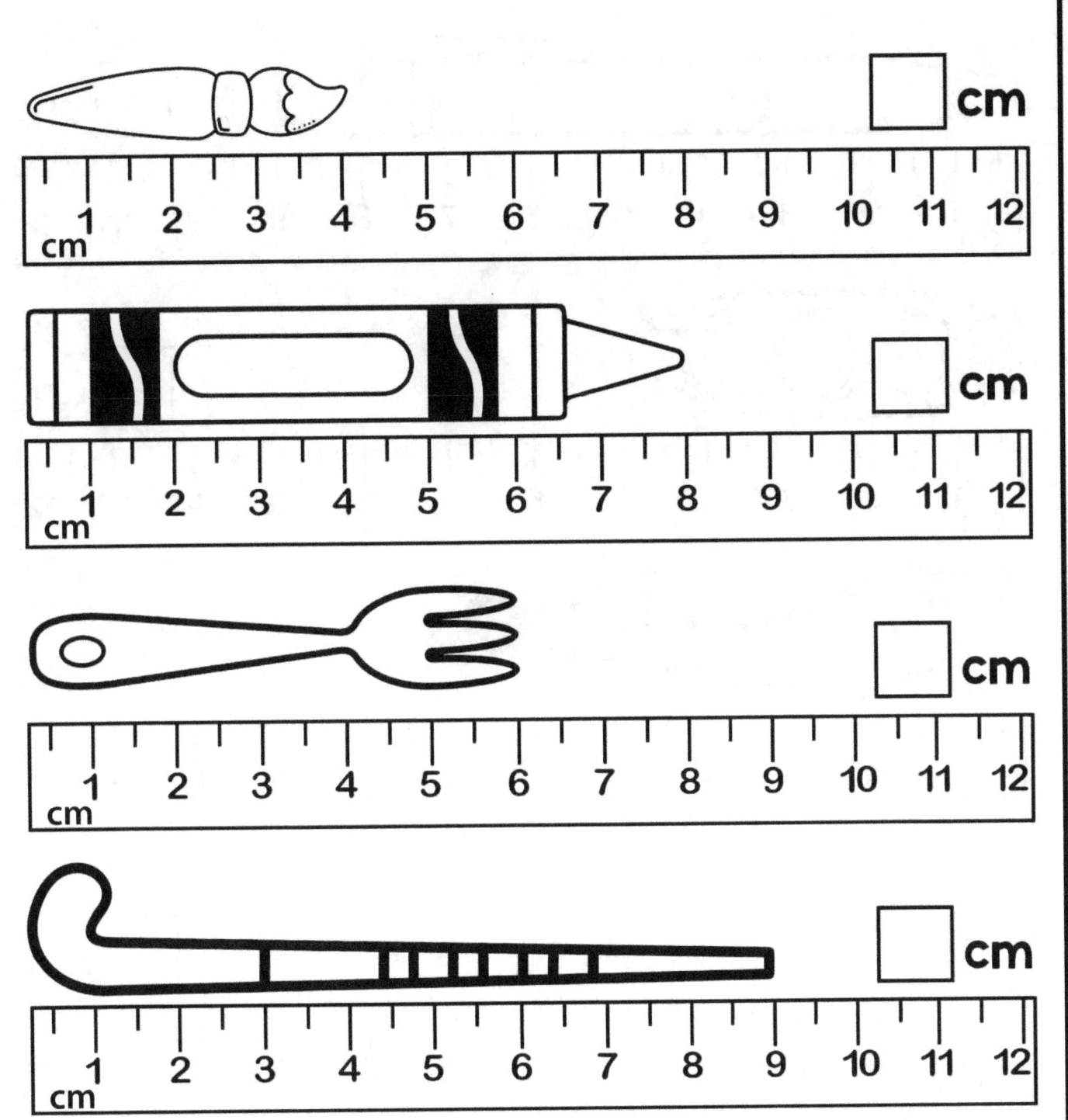

MEASURING LENGTH

Directions: Color the ruler to show how long the items are, and write your answer in the box.

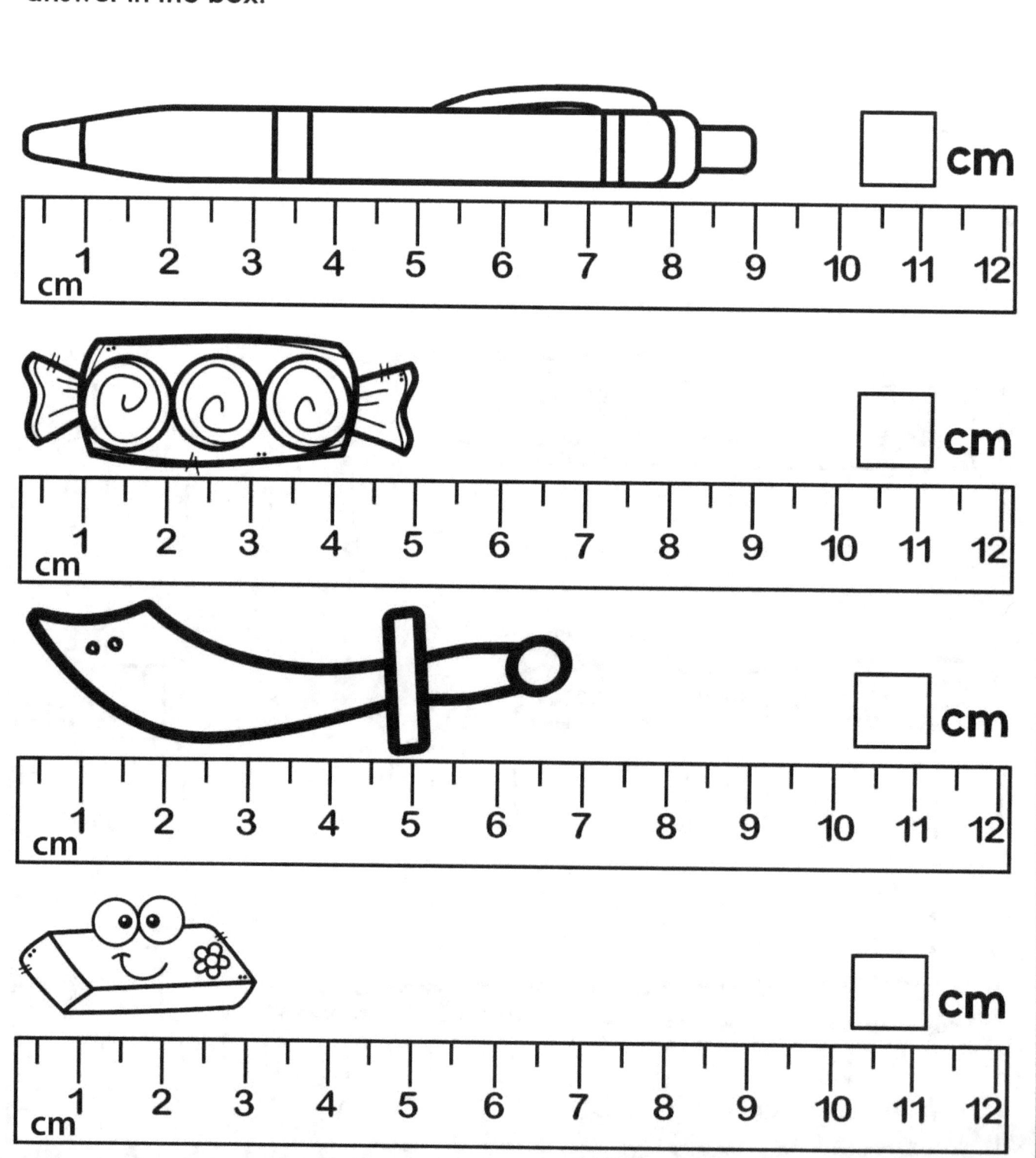

MEASURING LENGTH

Directions: Color the ruler to show how long the items are in centimeters.

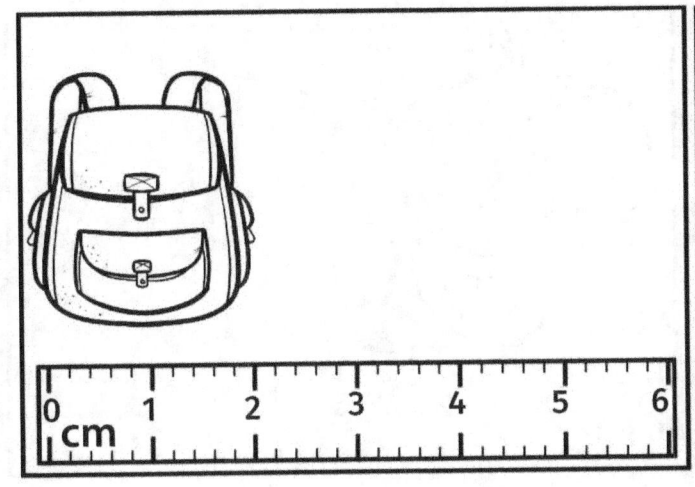

0 cm 1 2 3 4 5 6

0 cm 1 2 3 4 5 6

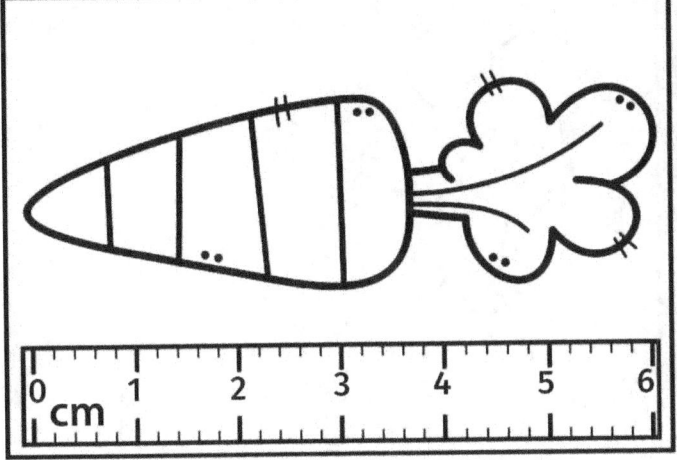

0 cm 1 2 3 4 5 6

0 cm 1 2 3 4 5 6

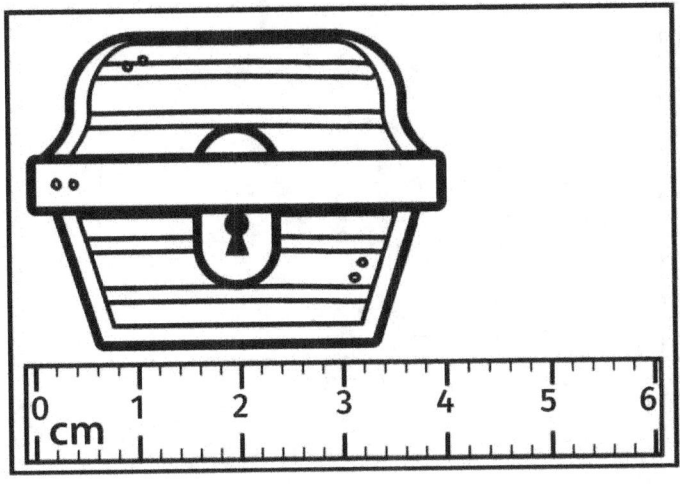

0 cm 1 2 3 4 5 6

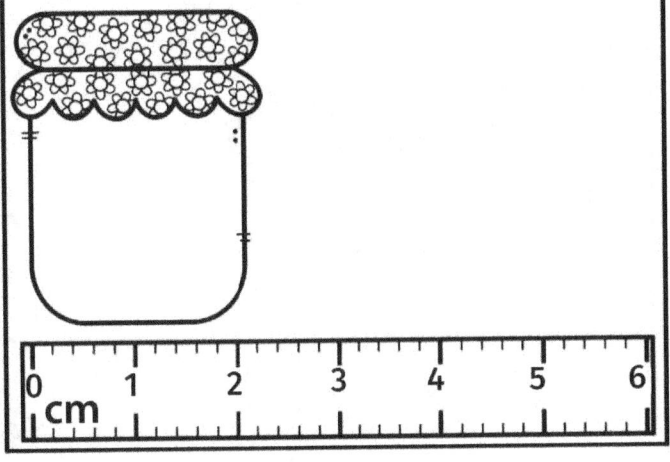

0 cm 1 2 3 4 5 6

MEASURING LENGTH

Directions: Color the ruler to show how long the items are in centimeters.

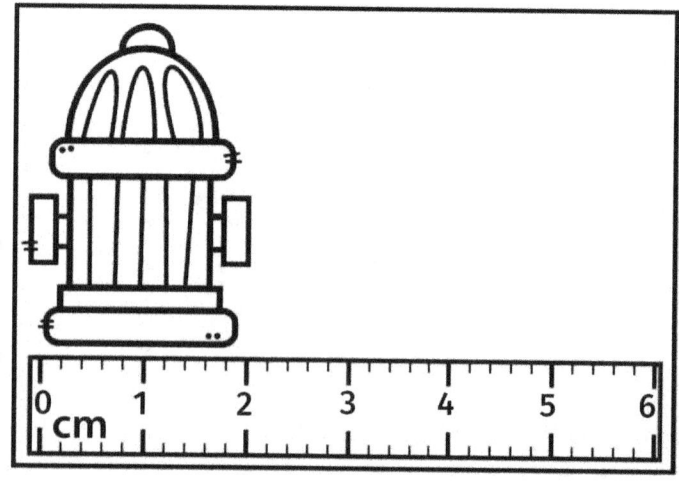

0 cm 1 2 3 4 5 6

0 cm 1 2 3 4 5 6

0 cm 1 2 3 4 5 6

0 cm 1 2 3 4 5 6

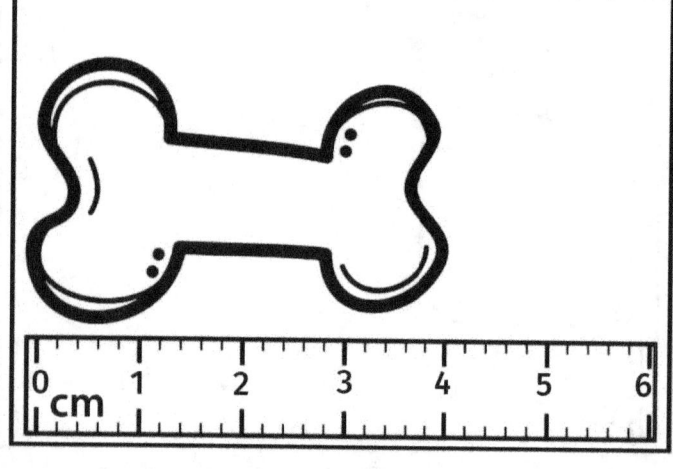

0 cm 1 2 3 4 5 6

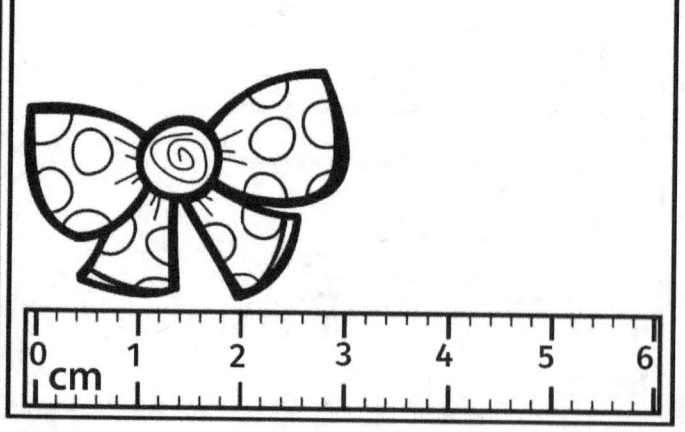

0 cm 1 2 3 4 5 6

MEASURING LENGTH

Directions: Color the ruler to the correct inches.

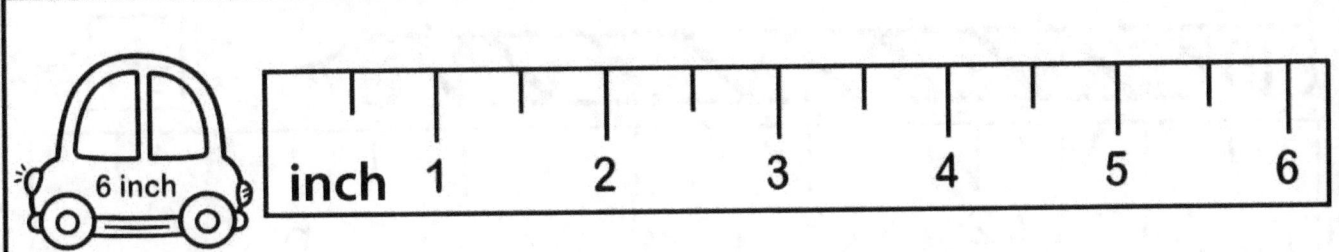

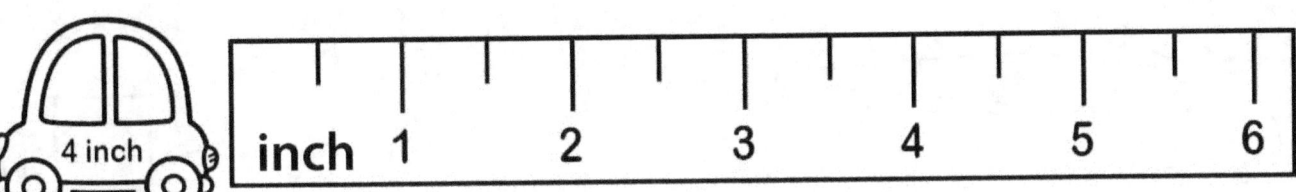

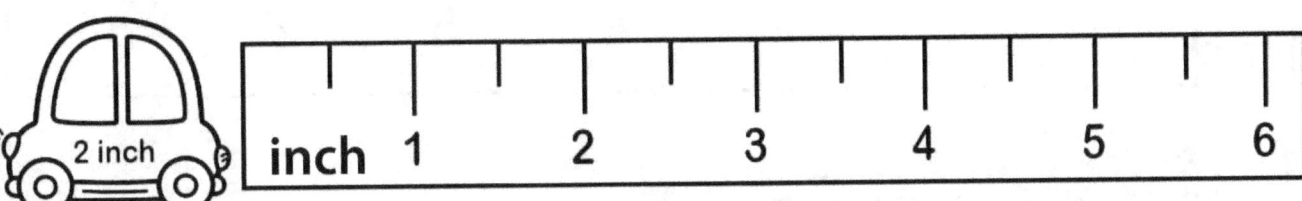

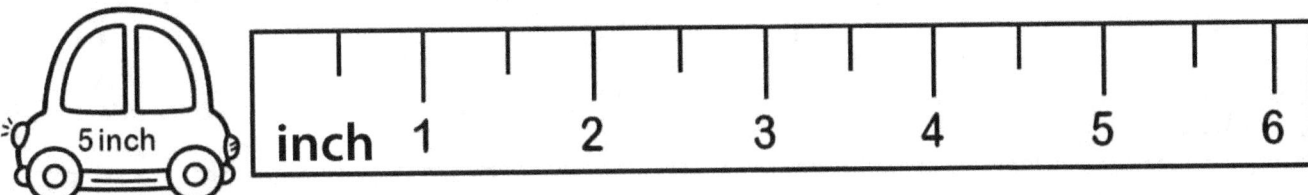

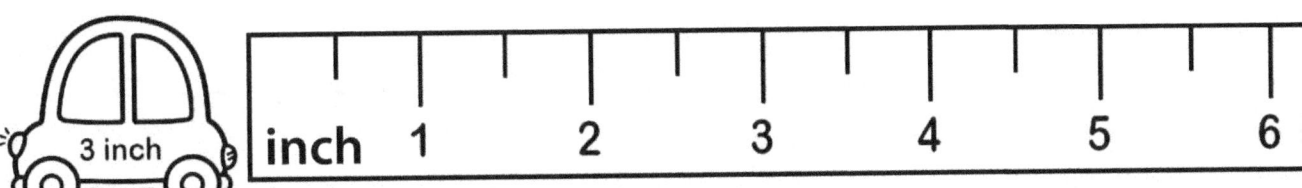

MEASURING LENGTH

Directions: Color the ruler to show how long the items are, and write your answer in the box.

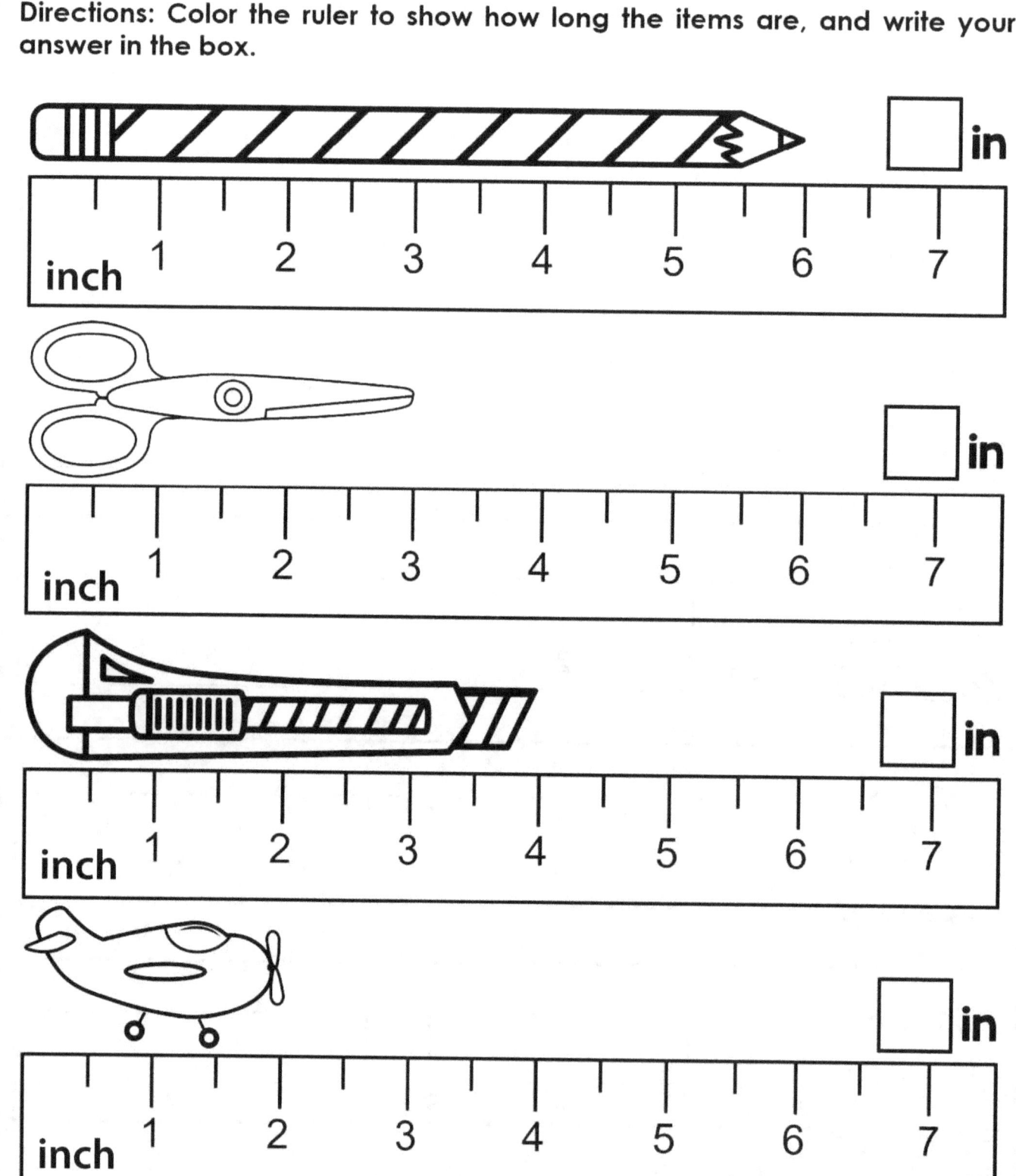

MEASURING LENGTH

Directions: Color the ruler to show how long the items are, and write your answer in the box.

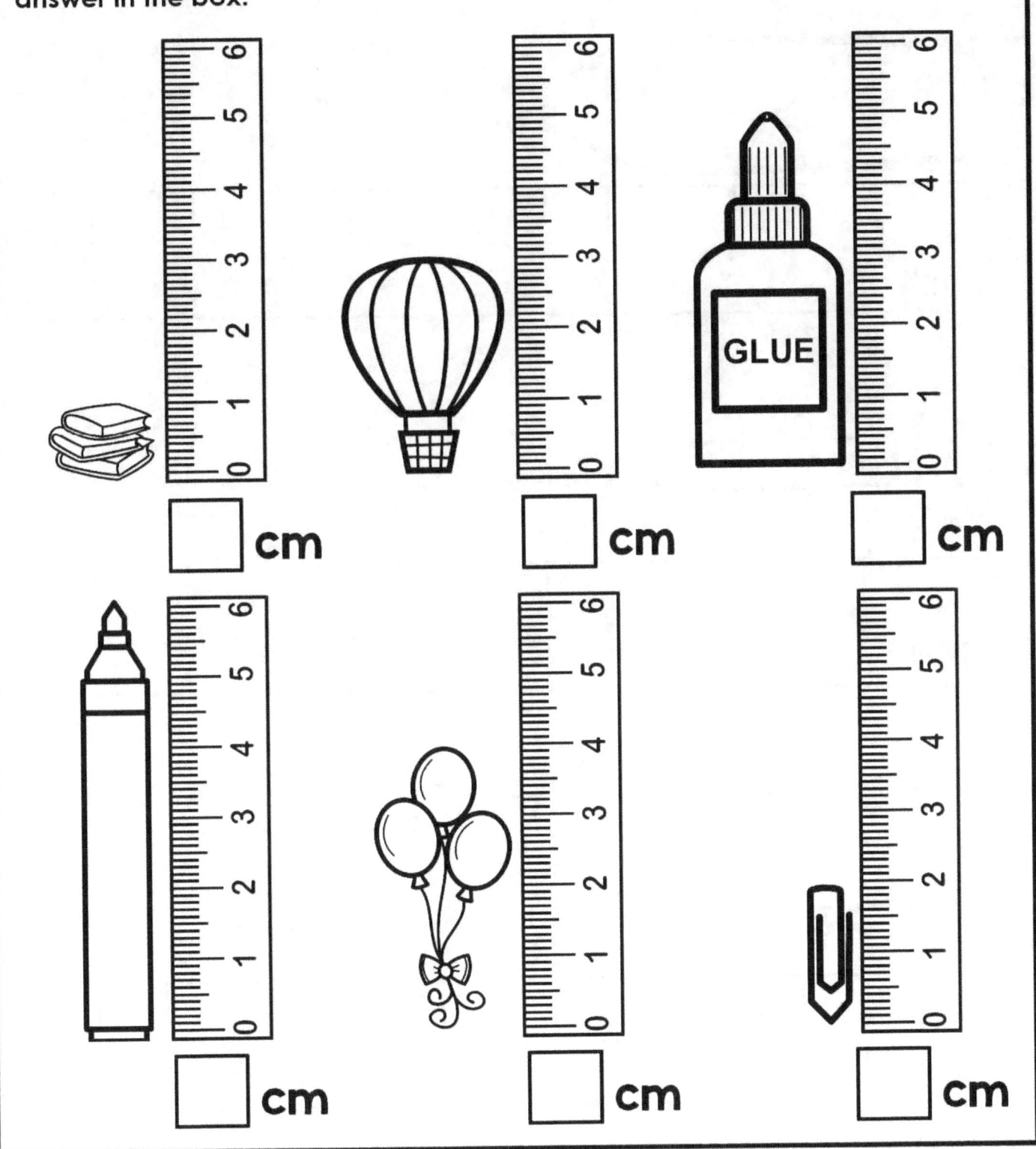

MEASURING LENGTH

Directions: Color the ruler to show how long the items are in inches.

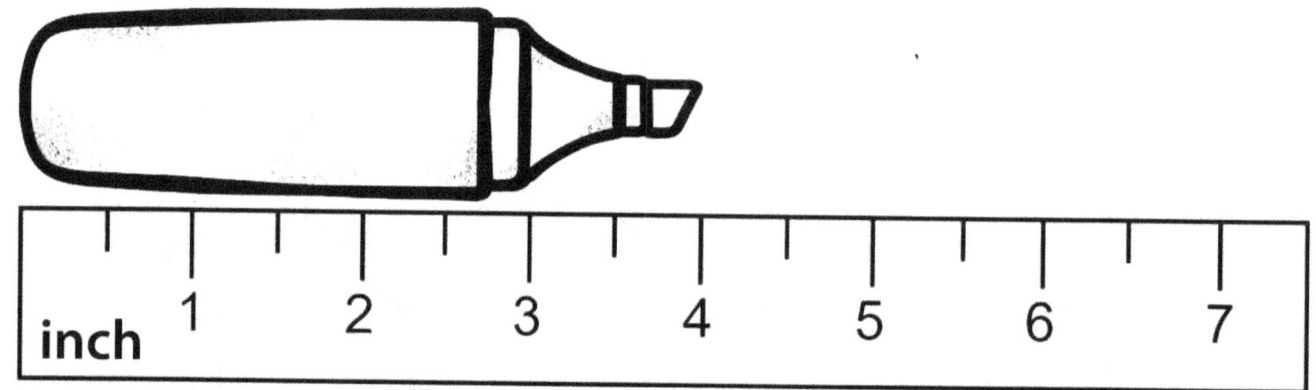

| inch | 1 | 2 | 3 | 4 | 5 | 6 | 7 |

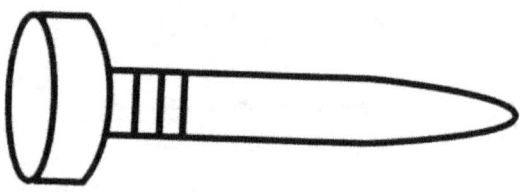

| inch | 1 | 2 | 3 | 4 | 5 | 6 | 7 |

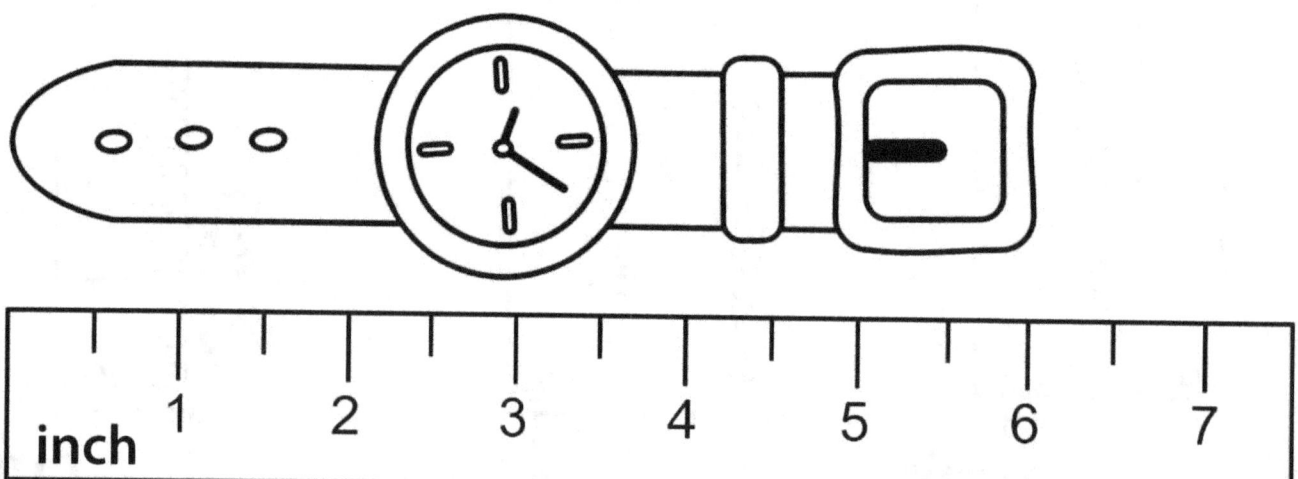

| inch | 1 | 2 | 3 | 4 | 5 | 6 | 7 |

MEASURING WIDTH

Directions: Count and color how many cubes wide each object is.

MEASURING WIDTH

Directions: Count and color how many cubes wide each object is.

MEASURING WIDTH

Directions: Color the widest object in each row.

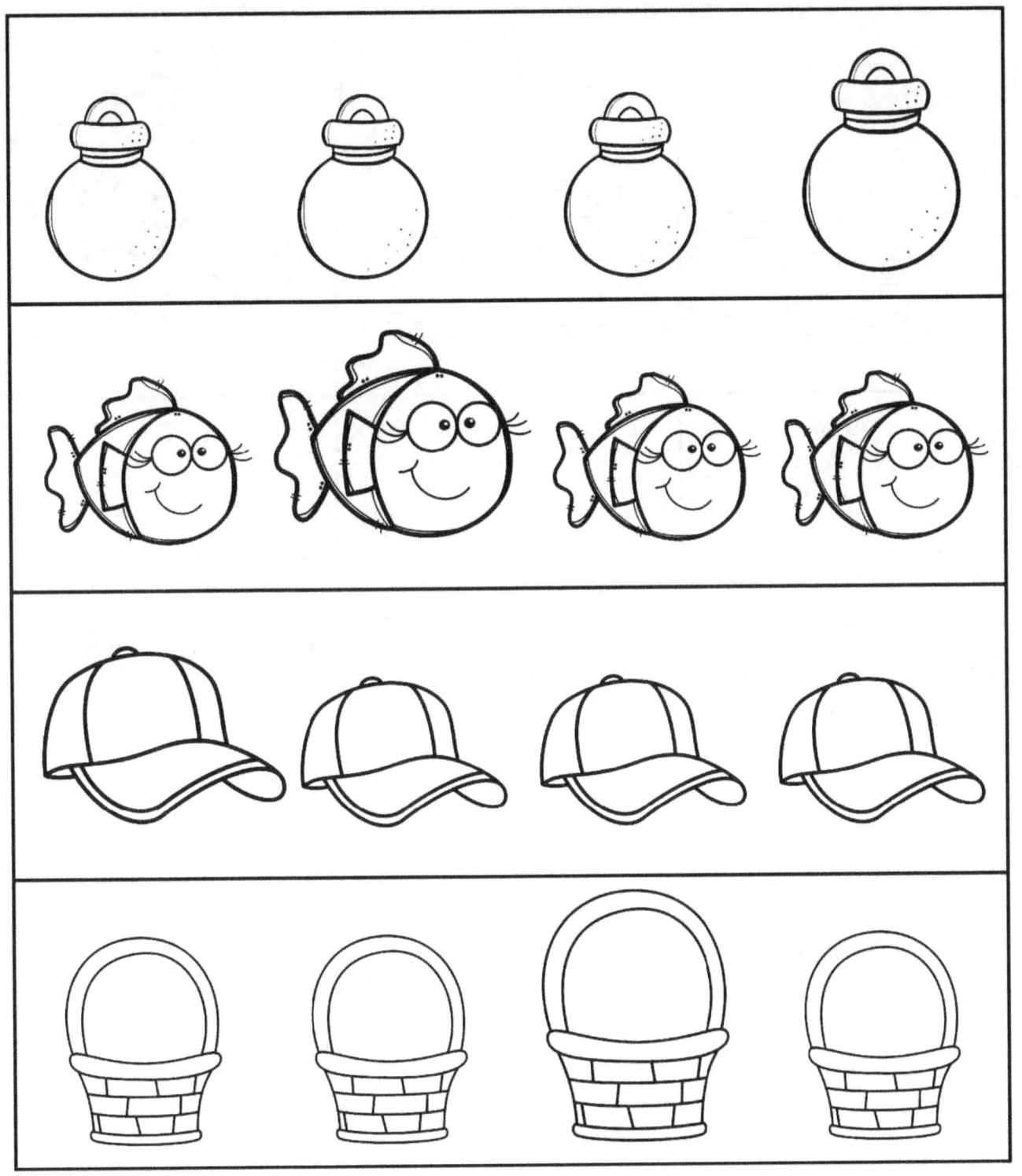

MEASURING WIDTH

Directions: Color the widest item in blue and color the narrow item in green.

MEASURING WIDTH

Directions: Color the widest item in blue and color the narrow item in green.

MEASURING WIDTH

Directions: Color the widest object in each row.

MEASURING WIDTH

Directions: Color the objects that are wider.

MEASURING CAPACITY

Directions: Color the object that is full.

Directions: Color the object that is empty.

MEASURING CAPACITY

Directions: Color the object that has the greatest capacity.

MEASURING CAPACITY

Directions: Color the object that has the least capacity.

MEASURING CAPACITY

Directions: Circle the object that has the greatest capacity in each row.

MEASURING CAPACITY

Directions: Color the object that has less capacity.

MEASURING CAPACITY

Directions: Color the liquid in each glass.

Almost Half

Empty

Full

Almost Empty

Almost Full

Half Empty

MEASURING CAPACITY

Directions: Draw and color the correct amount of liquid in each bottle.

Almost Empty	Full
Empty	Almost Full
Half Empty	Almost Half

MEASURING CAPACITY

Directions: Draw a line from the object on the left which has LESS capacity to the object on the right that has MORE capacity.

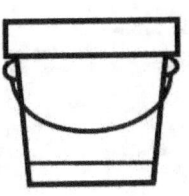   •   •

   •   •

   •   •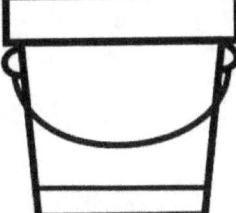

   •   •

   •   •

MEASURING VOLUME

Directions: Write the correct volume in the box.

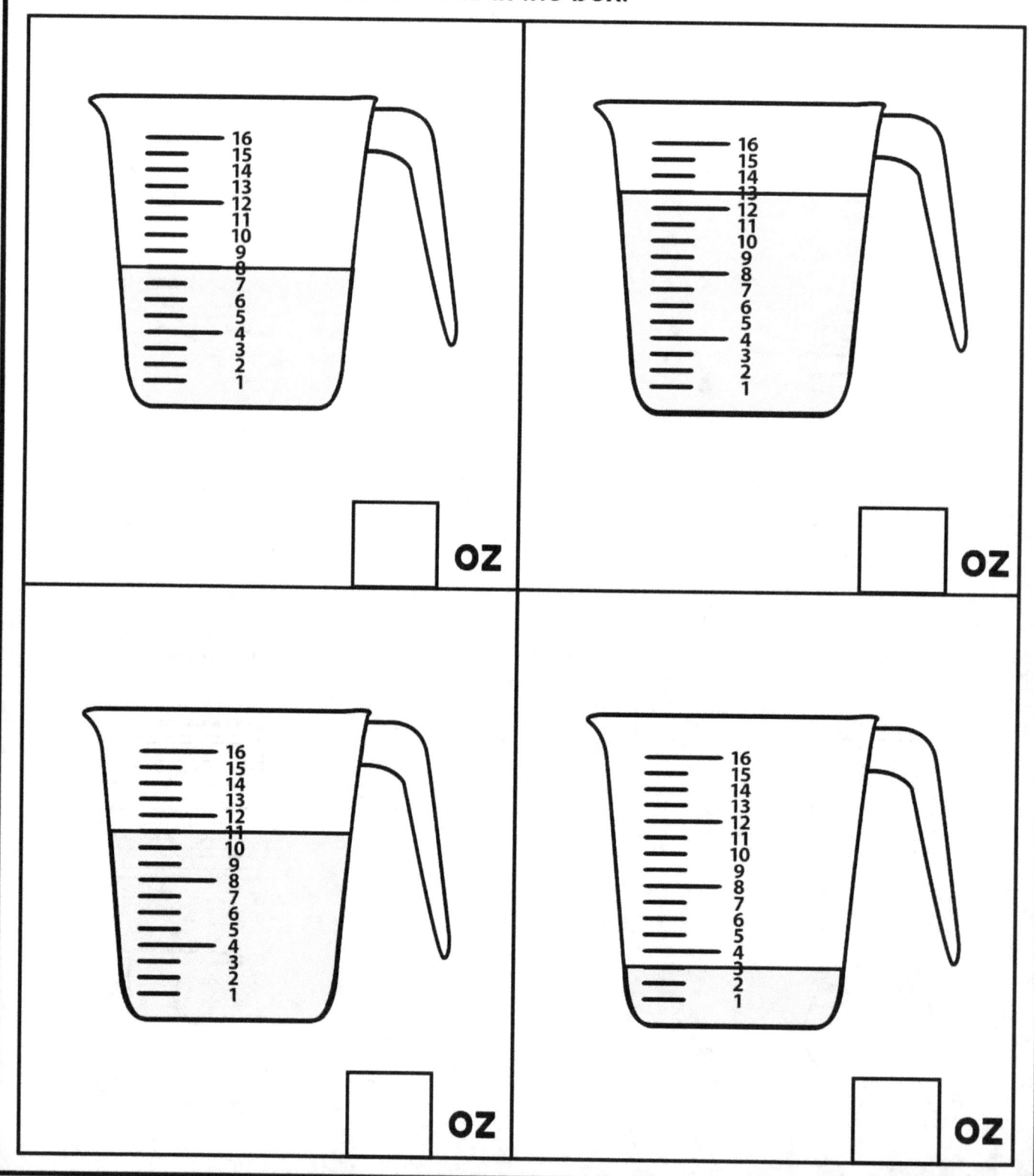

MEASURING VOLUME

Directions: Write the correct volume in the box.

MEASURING VOLUME

Directions: Write the correct volume in the box.

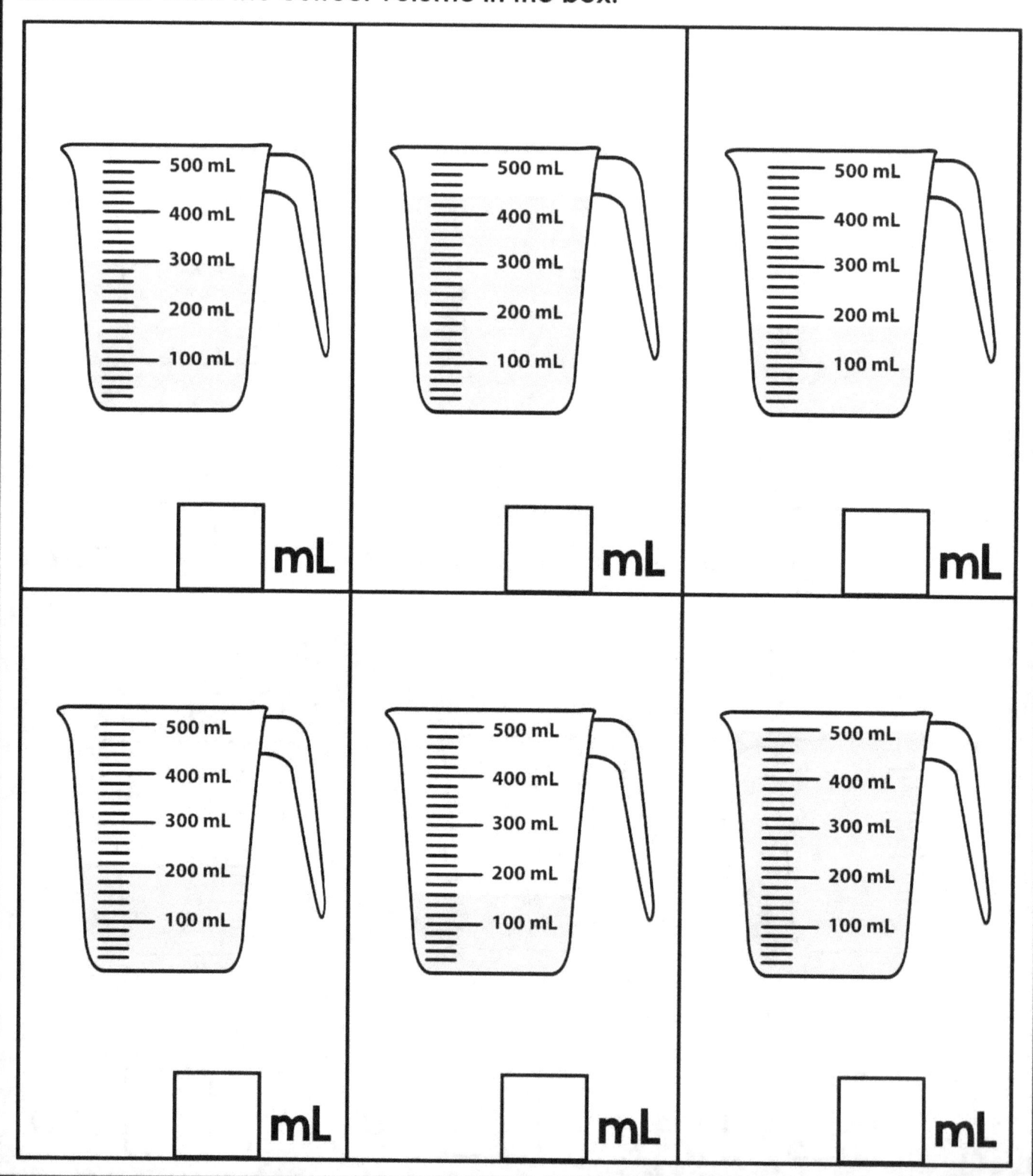

MEASURING VOLUME

Directions: Write the correct volume in the box.

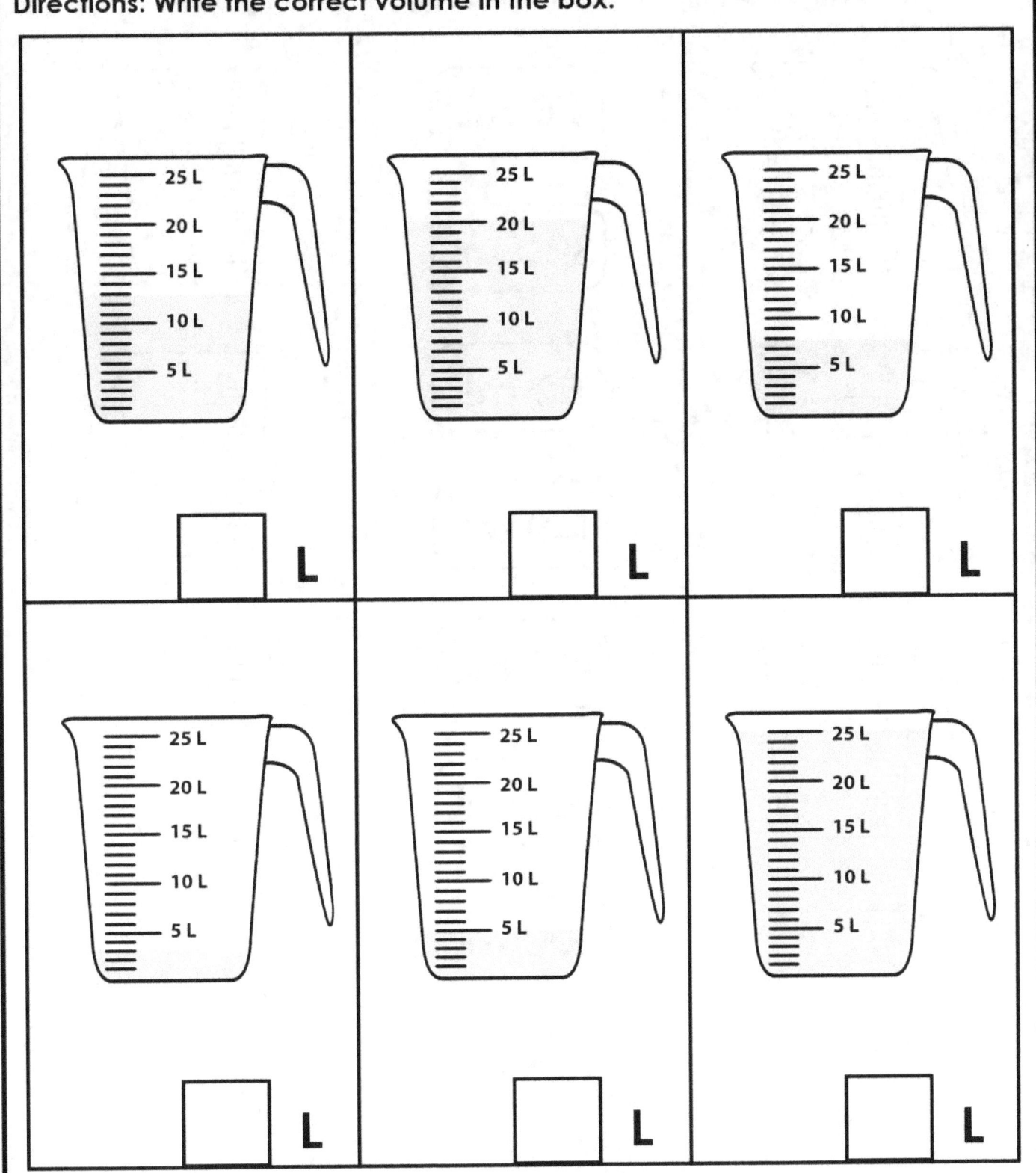

MEASURING VOLUME

Directions: Draw a line from the volume to correct measuring cup.

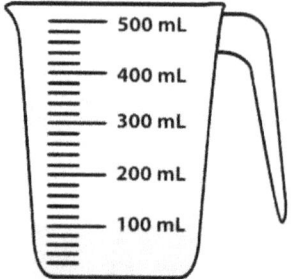

20 mL

300 mL

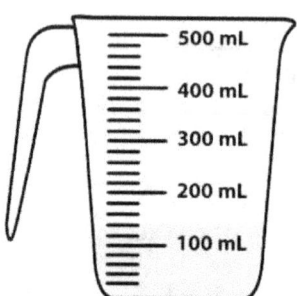
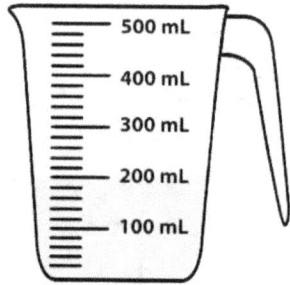

60 mL

140 mL

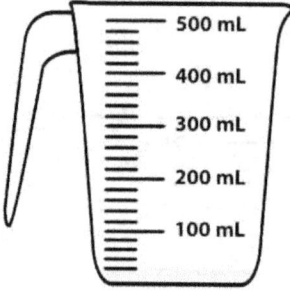
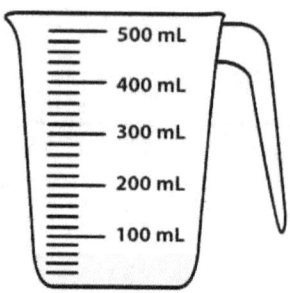

100 mL

500 mL

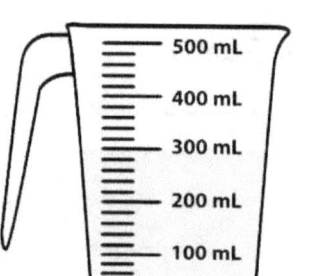

200 mL

380 mL

MEASURING VOLUME

Directions: Color the correct volume box.

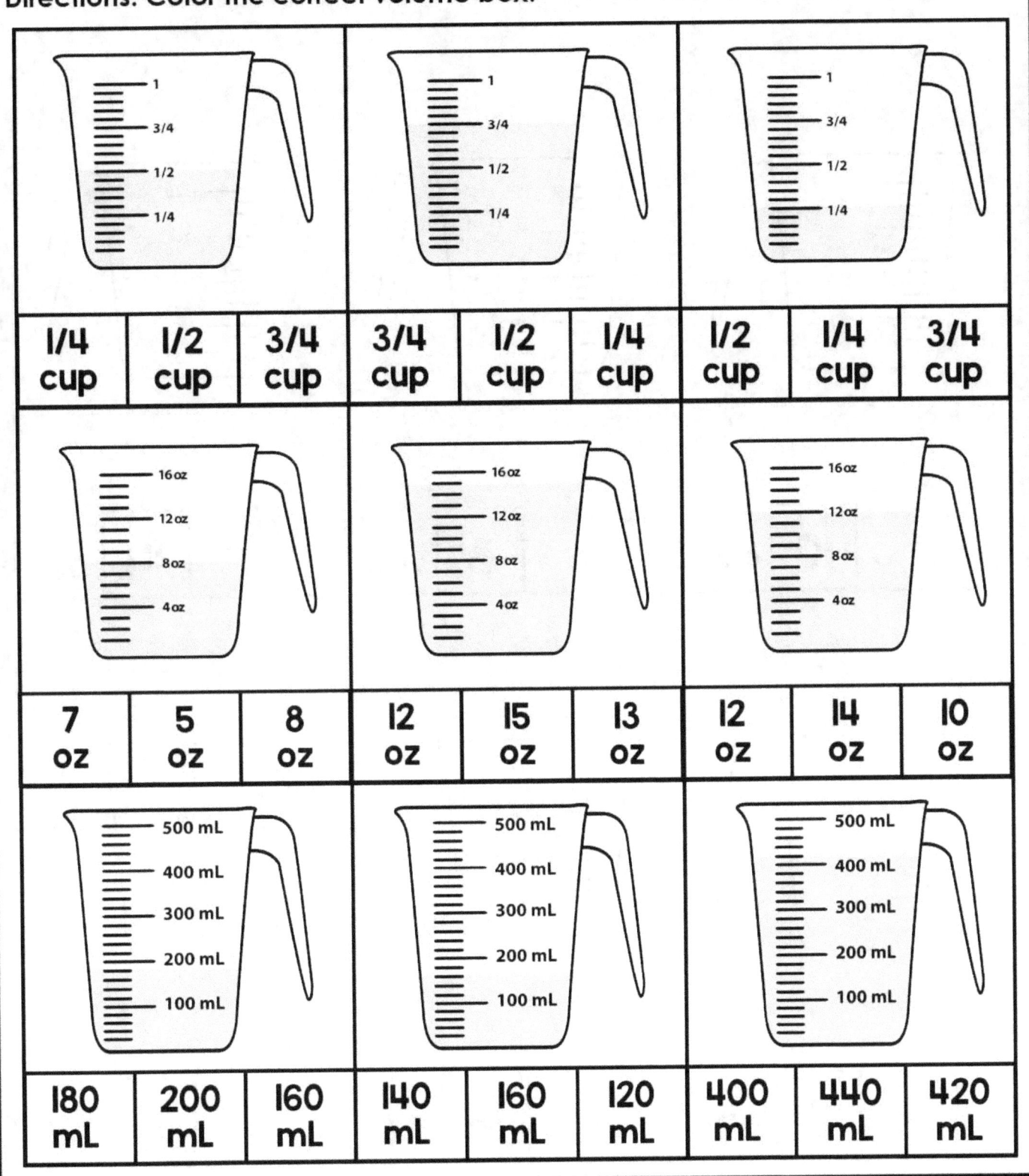

1/4 cup	1/2 cup	3/4 cup	3/4 cup	1/2 cup	1/4 cup	1/2 cup	1/4 cup	3/4 cup

7 oz	5 oz	8 oz	12 oz	15 oz	13 oz	12 oz	14 oz	10 oz

180 mL	200 mL	160 mL	140 mL	160 mL	120 mL	400 mL	440 mL	420 mL

MEASURING VOLUME

Directions: Color the measuring cup to the correct volume.

MEASURING VOLUME

Directions: Color the measuring cup to the correct volume.

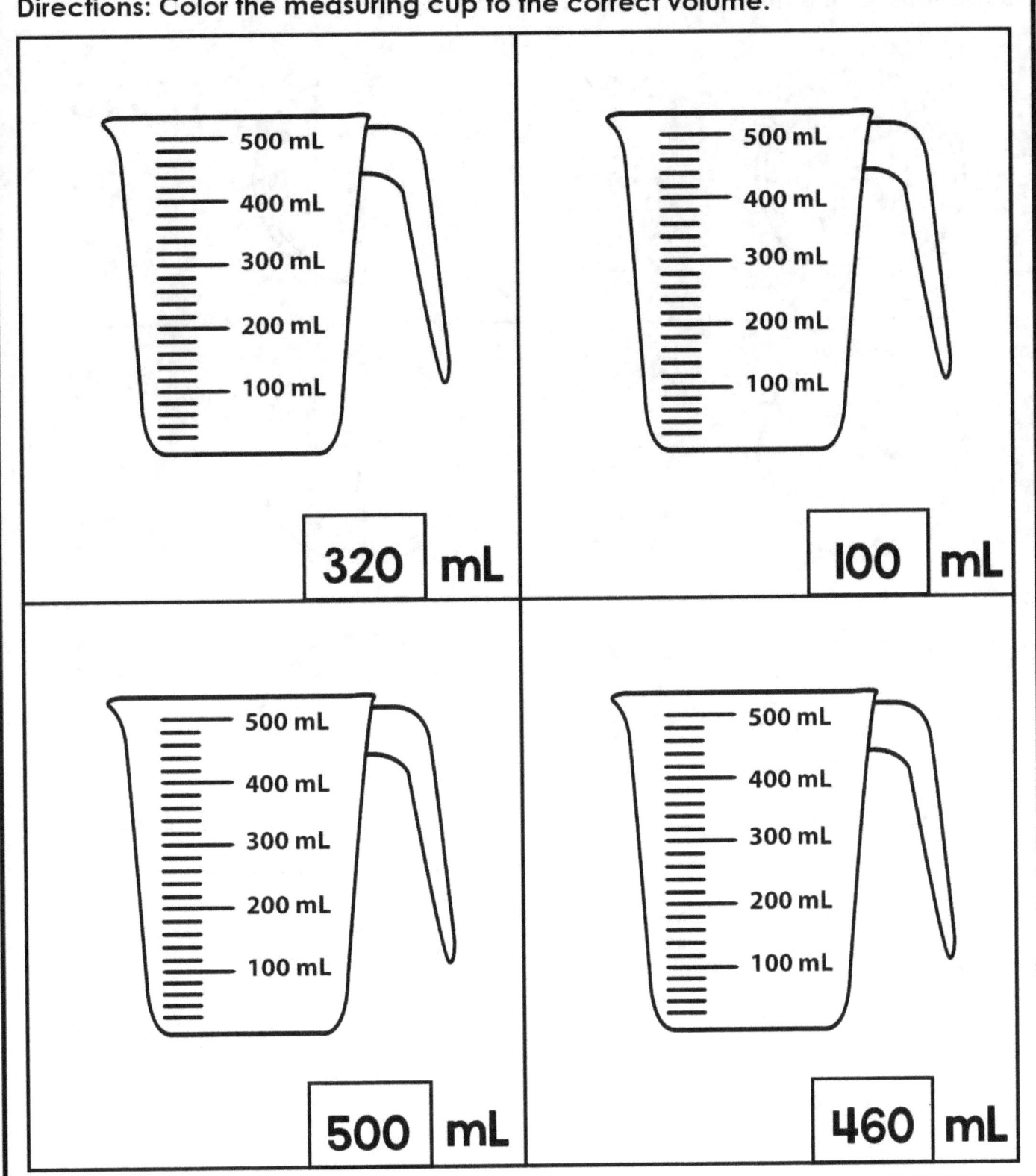

500 mL
400 mL
300 mL
200 mL
100 mL

320 mL

500 mL
400 mL
300 mL
200 mL
100 mL

100 mL

500 mL
400 mL
300 mL
200 mL
100 mL

500 mL

500 mL
400 mL
300 mL
200 mL
100 mL

460 mL

TELLING TIME

Directions: Circle the correct time shown on each clock.

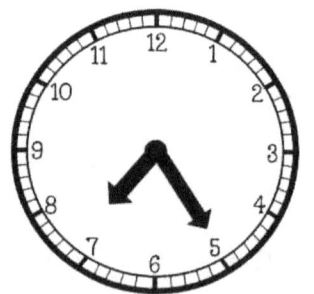

12:30

7:25

8:20

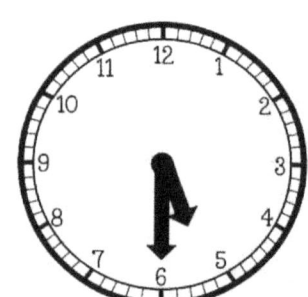

5:30

6:30

4:25

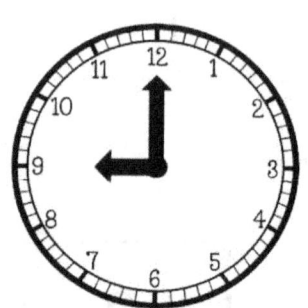

8:30

6:00

9:00

12:30

10:30

7:45

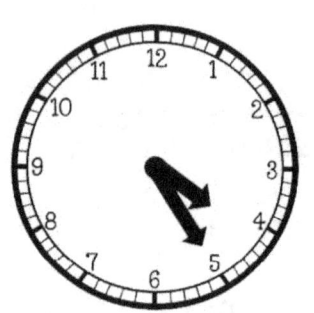

4:25

2:30

5:00

9:30

7:30

8:30

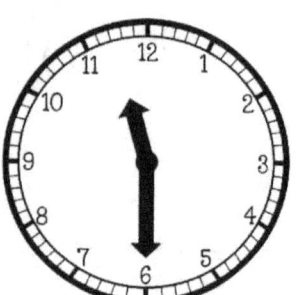

10:30

11:30

12:30

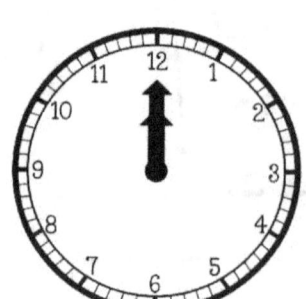

12:00

12:30

12:05

TELLING TIME

Directions: Draw a line from the time to the correct time on the clock face.

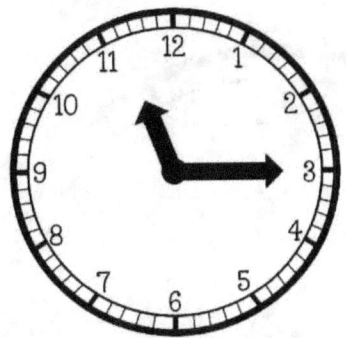
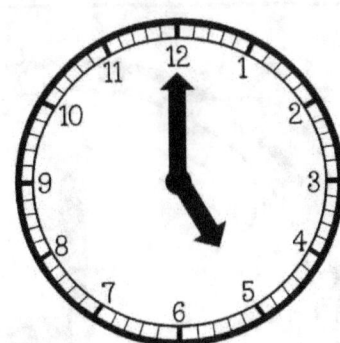

| 12:30 |
| 7:00 |
| 9:45 |
| 5:00 |

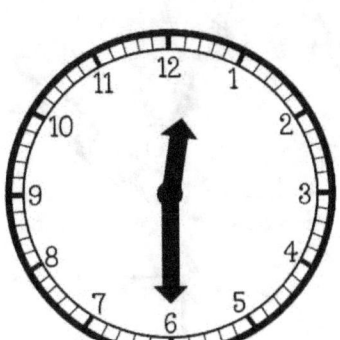

| 8:30 |
| 11:15 |

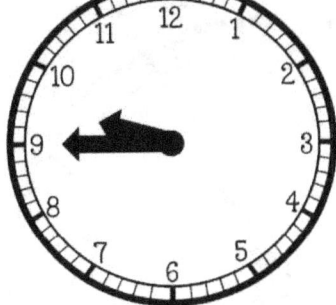

| 6:30 |
| 10:00 |

TELLING TIME

Directions: Write the correct time in the box.

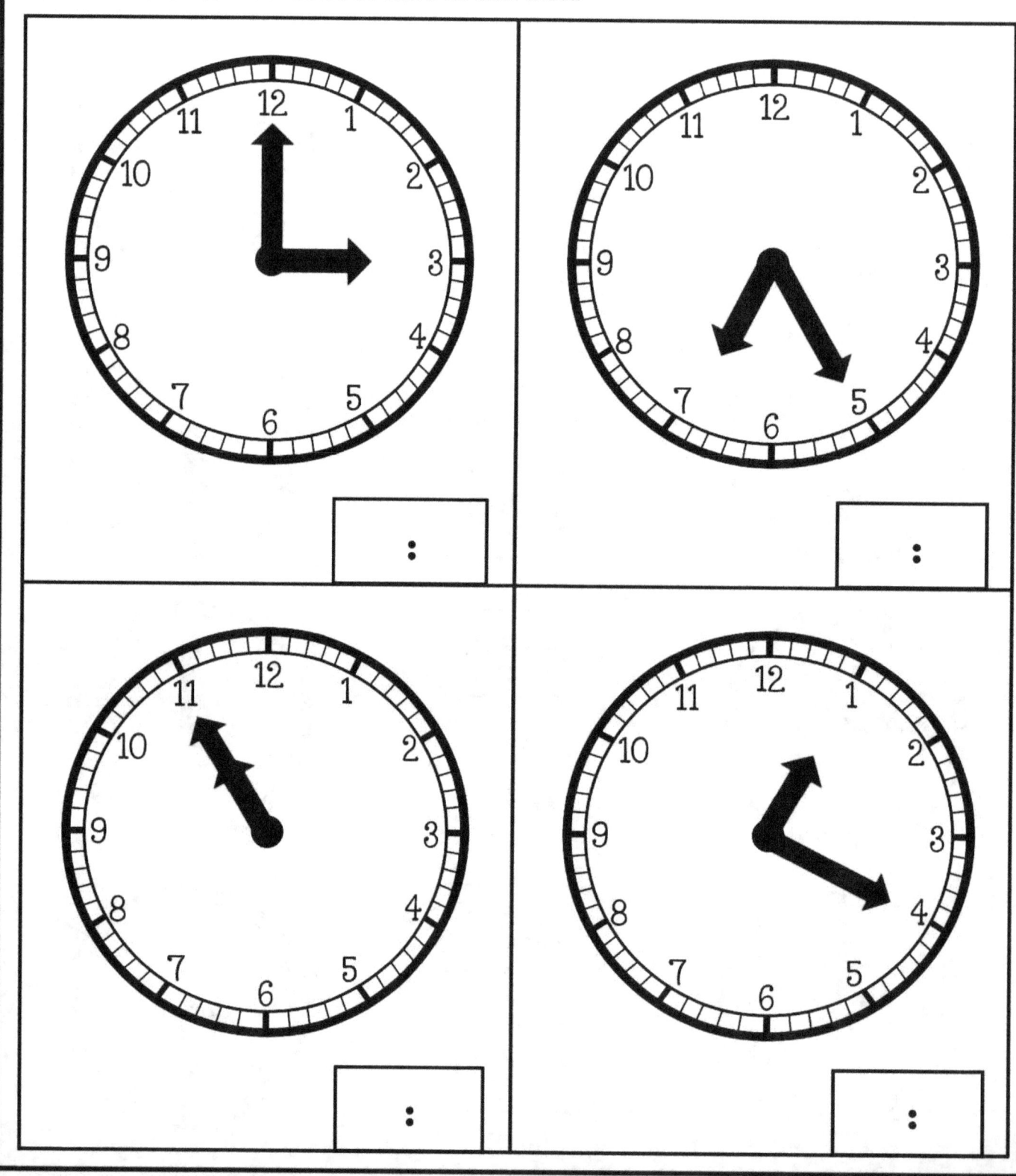

TELLING TIME

Directions: Write the correct time in the box.

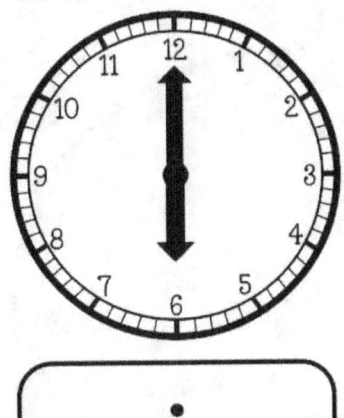

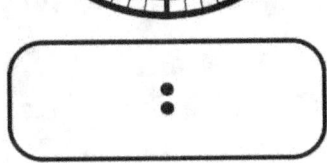

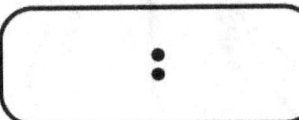

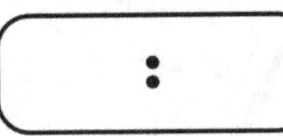

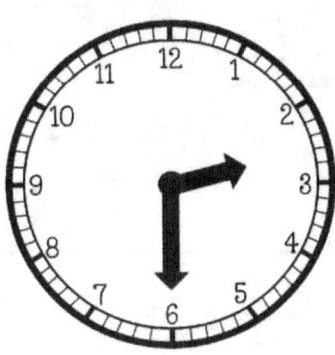

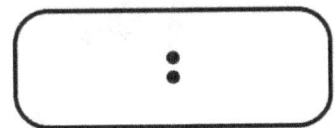

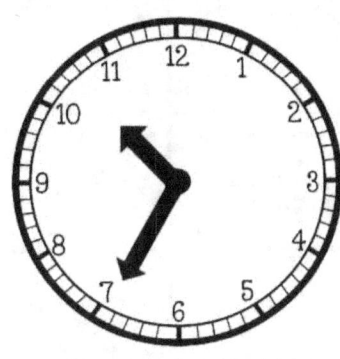

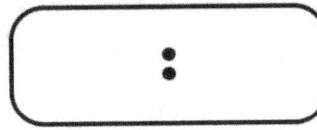

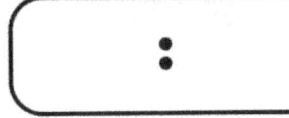

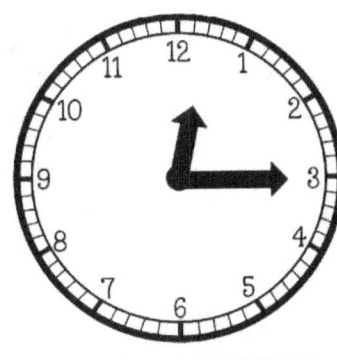

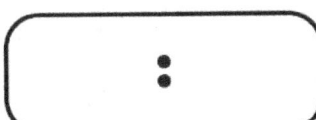

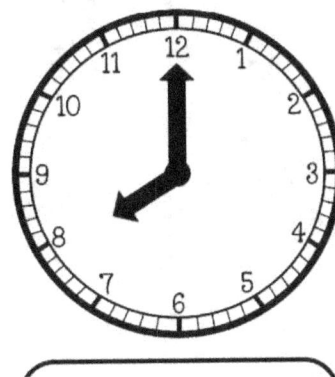

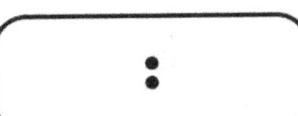

TELLING TIME

Directions: Draw hands on the clock face to show the time.

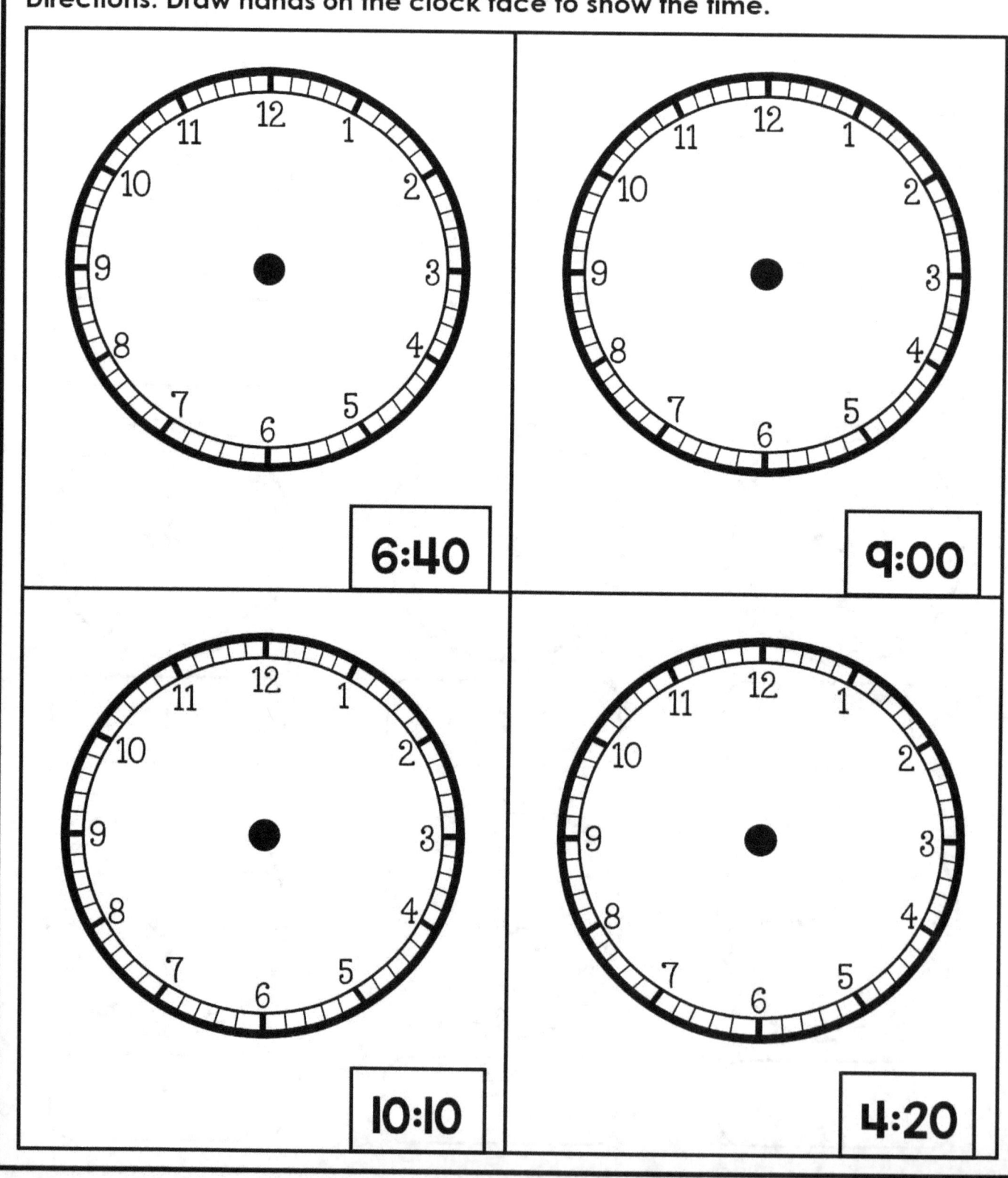

6:40

9:00

10:10

4:20

TELLING TIME

Directions: Draw hands on the clock face to show the time.

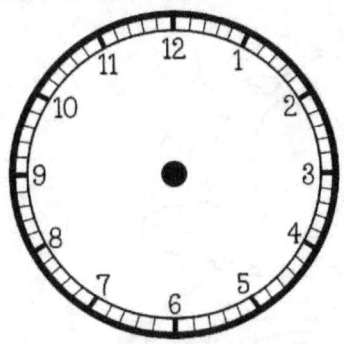

6:45

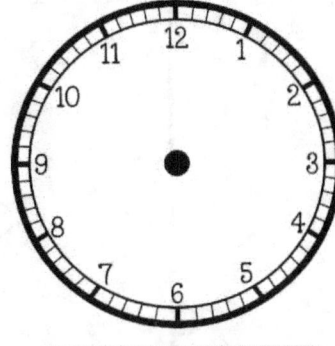

2:00

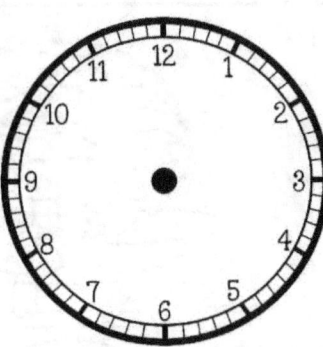

5:15

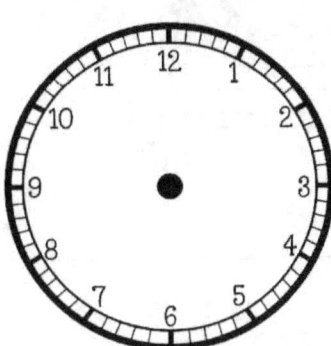

1:30

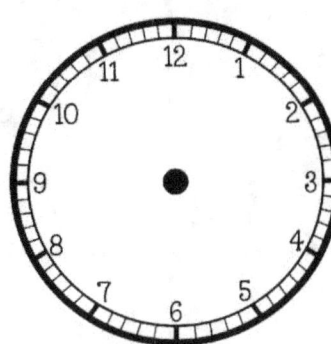

4:00

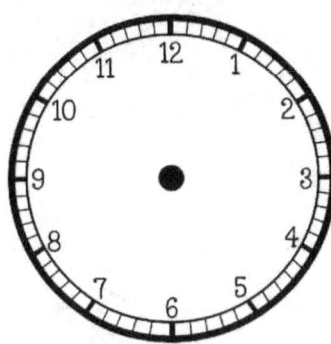

8:25

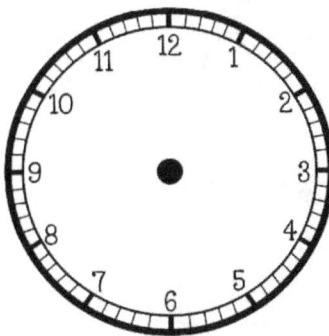

12:00

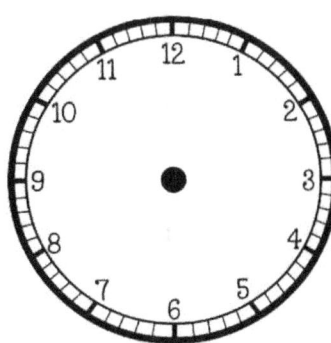

10:45

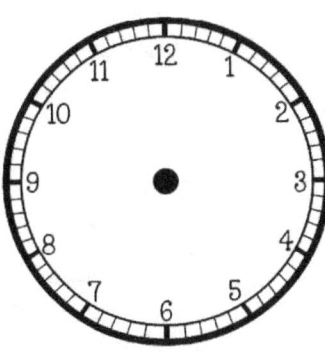

3:30

MEASURING WEIGHT

Directions: Write the correct weight in the box.

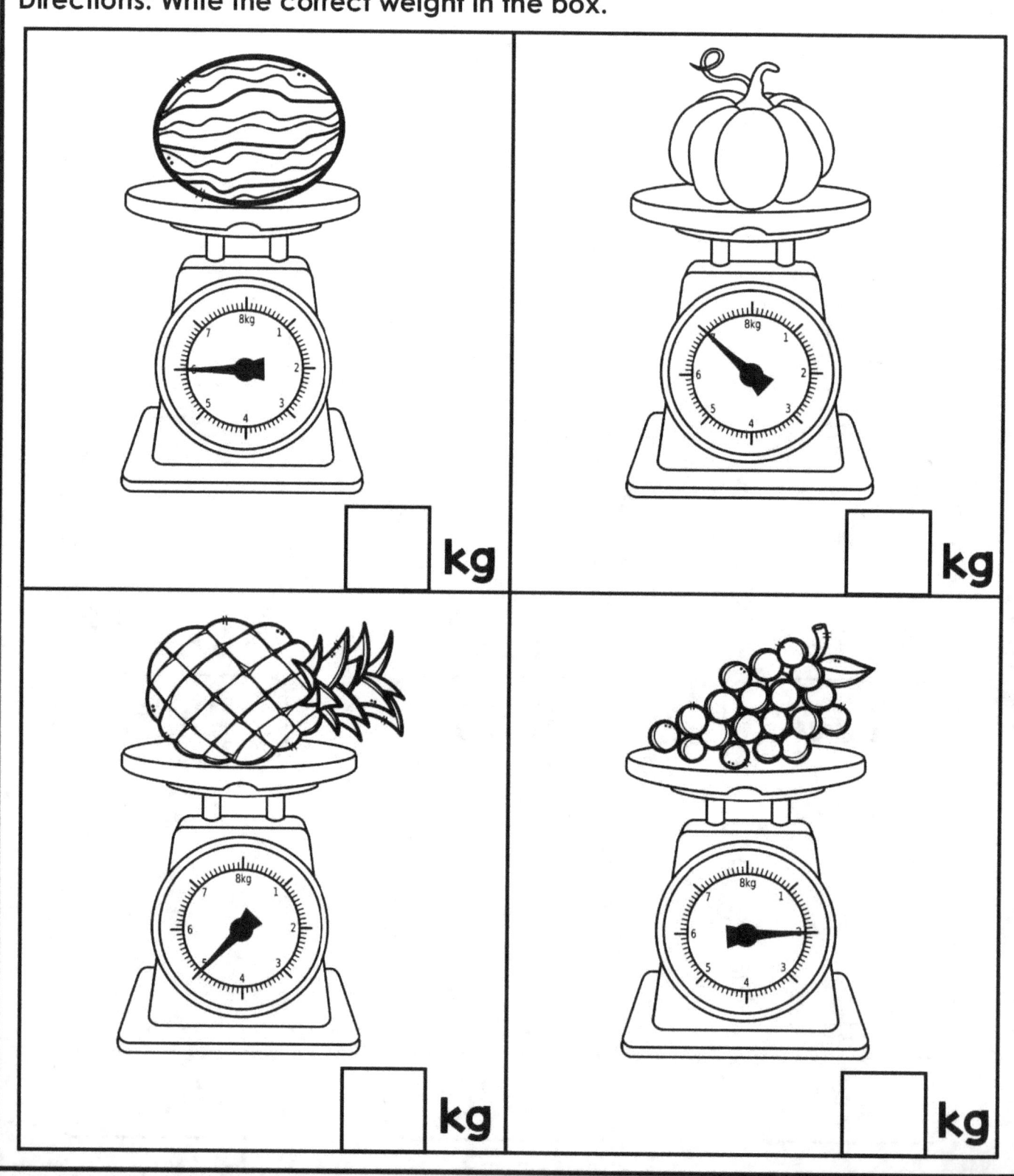

kg

kg

kg

kg

MEASURING WEIGHT

Directions: Write the correct weight in the box.

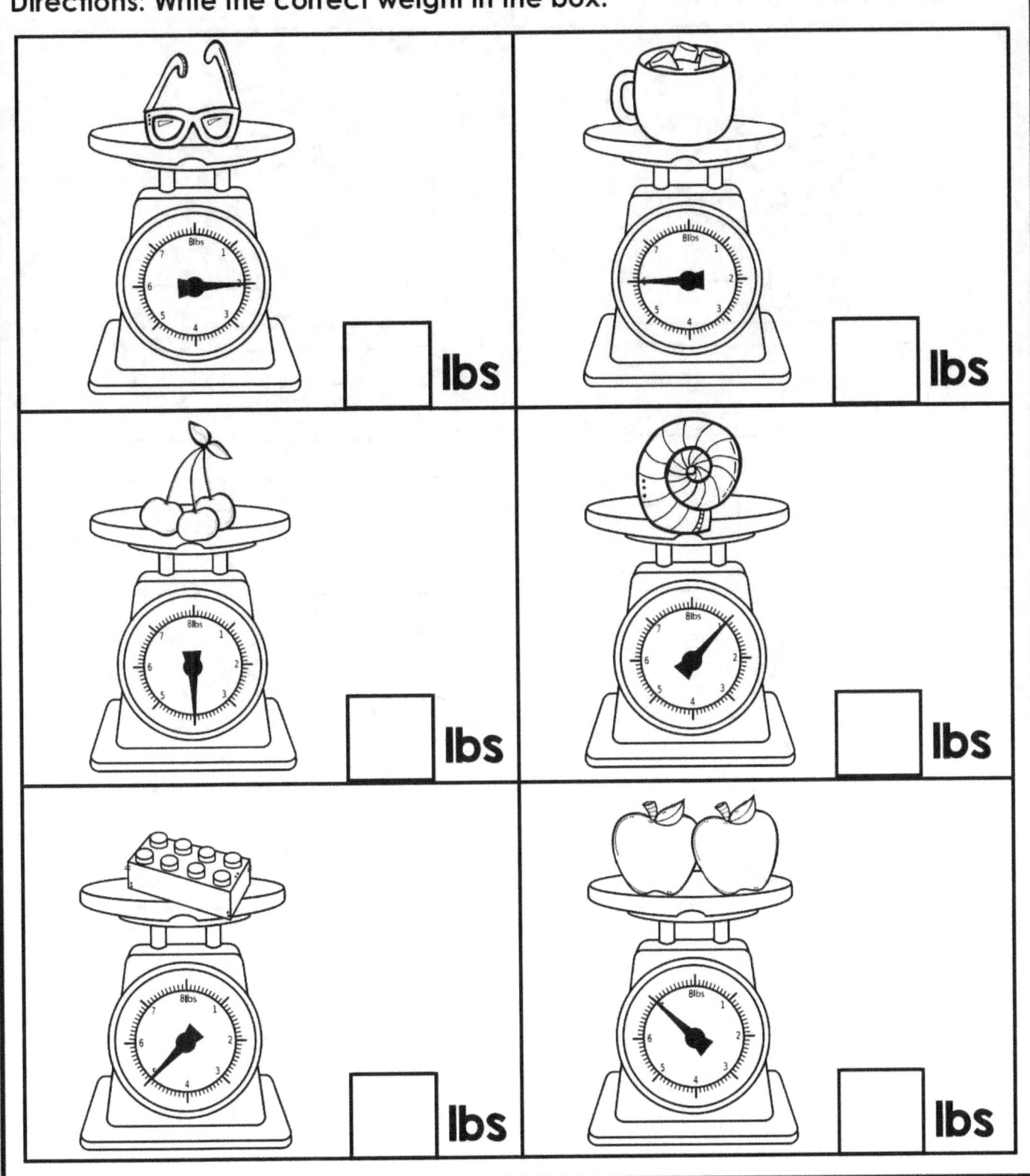

MEASURING WEIGHT

Directions: Write the correct weight in the box.

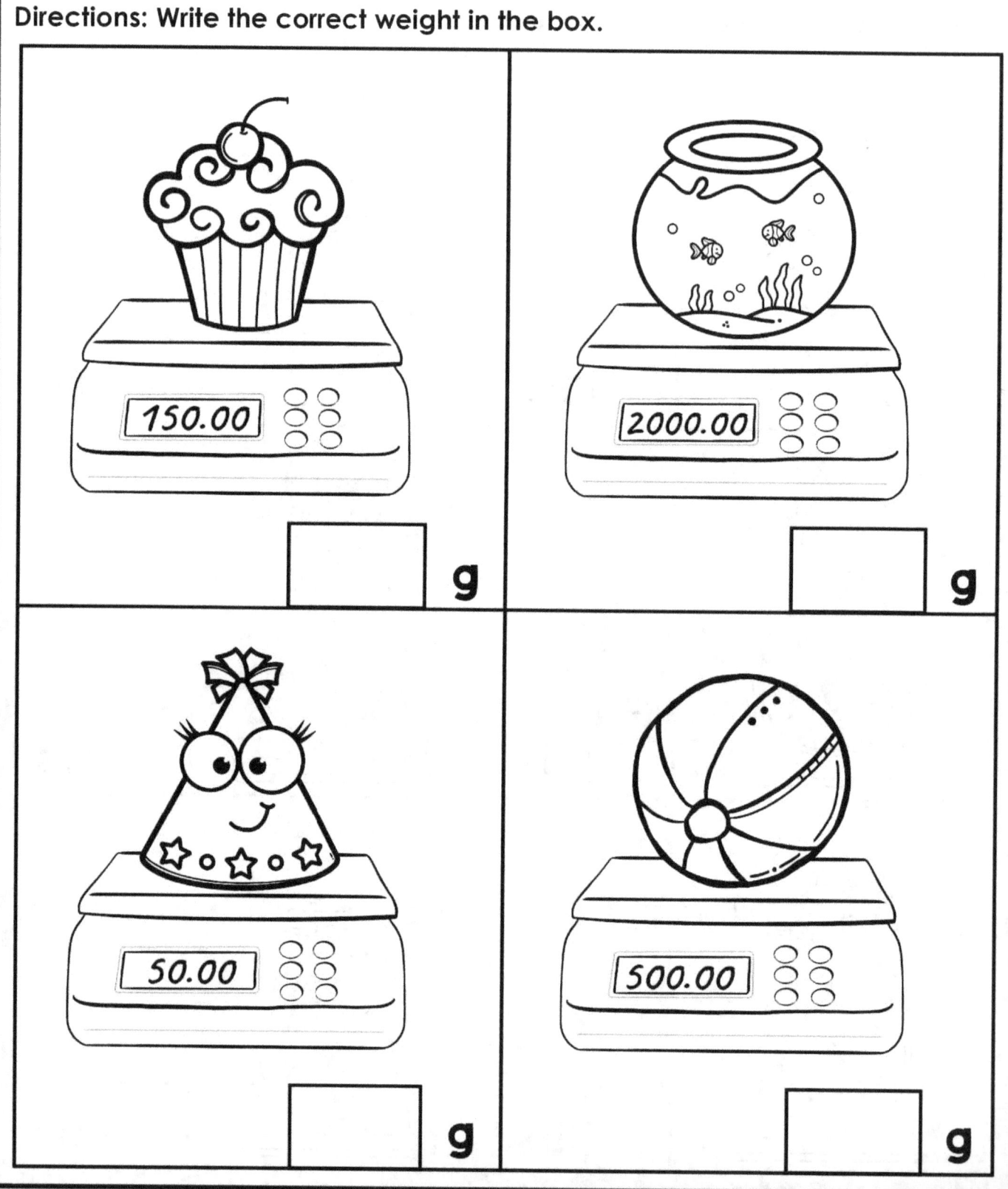

MEASURING WEIGHT

Directions: Add up the weights and write your answer in the box.

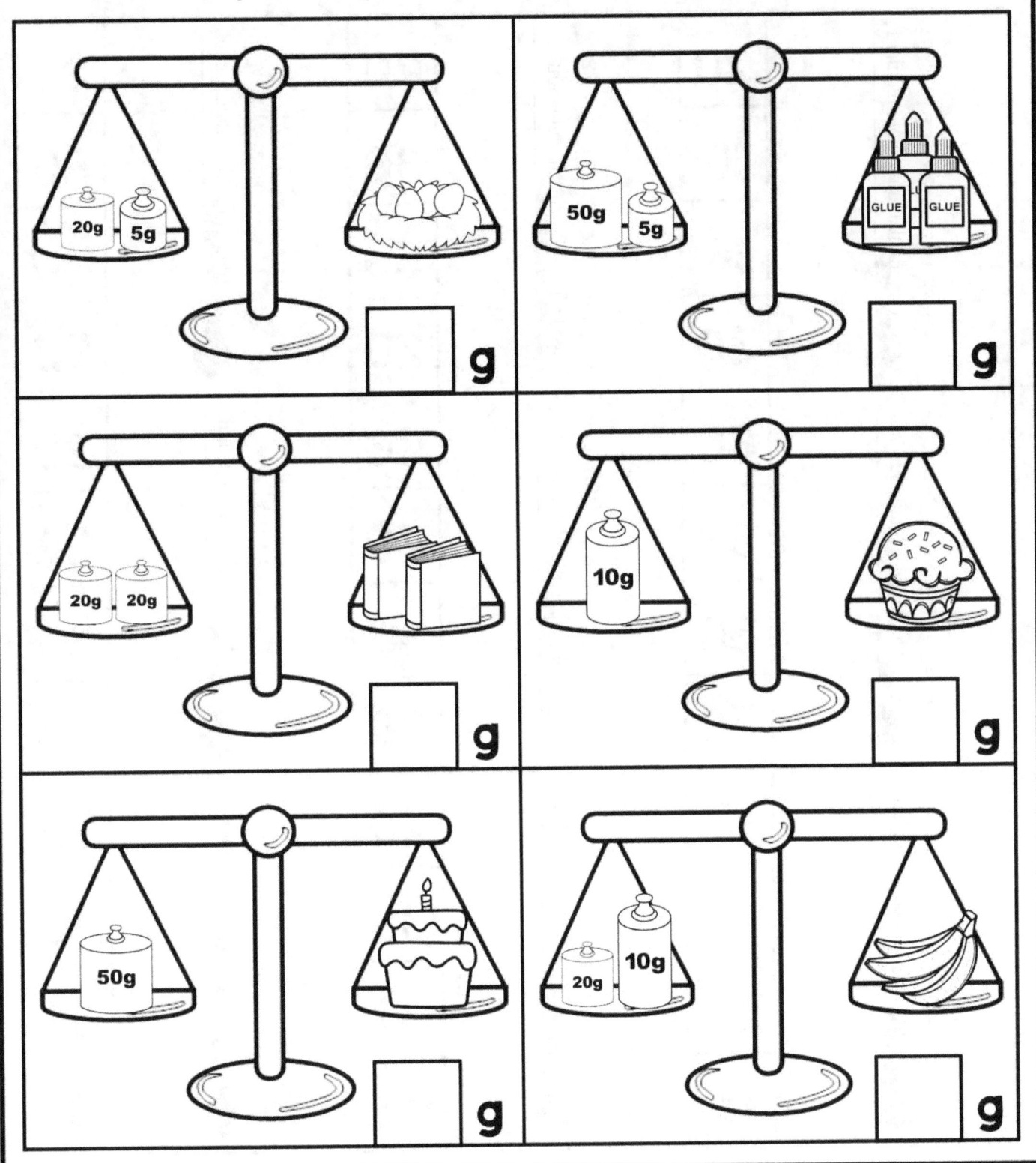

MEASURING TEMPERATURE

Directions: Color the correct temperature.

Thermometer	Options
100°, 90°, 80°, 70°, 60°, 50°, 40°, 30°, 20°, 10°, 0°	20 / 10 / 16 / 30
100°, 90°, 80°, 70°, 60°, 50°, 40°, 30°, 20°, 10°, 0°	40 / 36 / 50 / 20
100°, 90°, 80°, 70°, 60°, 50°, 40°, 30°, 20°, 10°, 0°	30 / 50 / 40 / 52
100°, 90°, 80°, 70°, 60°, 50°, 40°, 30°, 20°, 10°, 0°	50 / 60 / 56 / 58
100°, 90°, 80°, 70°, 60°, 50°, 40°, 30°, 20°, 10°, 0°	46 / 40 / 30 / 38
100°, 90°, 80°, 70°, 60°, 50°, 40°, 30°, 20°, 10°, 0°	20 / 32 / 30 / 28
100°, 90°, 80°, 70°, 60°, 50°, 40°, 30°, 20°, 10°, 0°	10 / 20 / 24 / 18
100°, 90°, 80°, 70°, 60°, 50°, 40°, 30°, 20°, 10°, 0°	40 / 38 / 42 / 46
100°, 90°, 80°, 70°, 60°, 50°, 40°, 30°, 20°, 10°, 0°	78 / 80 / 68 / 100

MEASURING TEMPERATURE

Directions: Write correct temperature in the box.

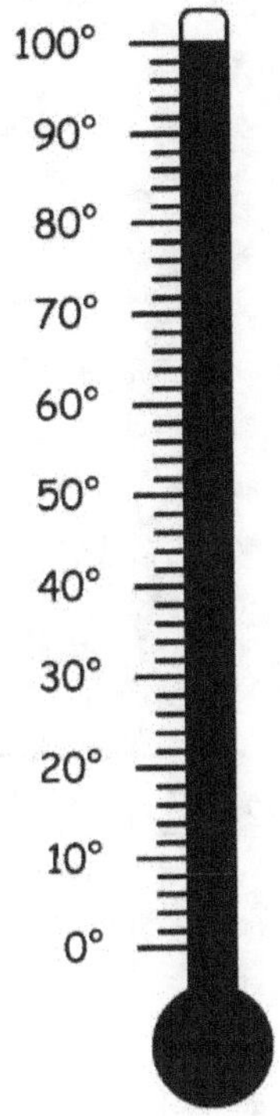

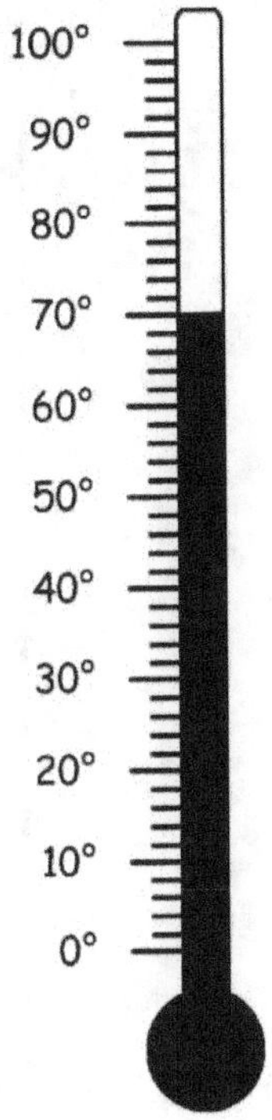

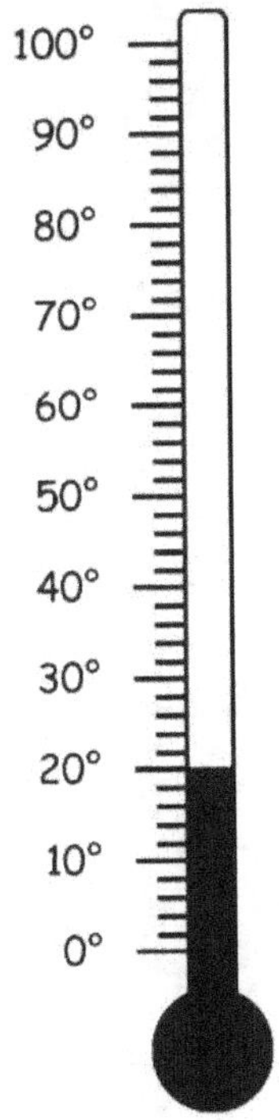

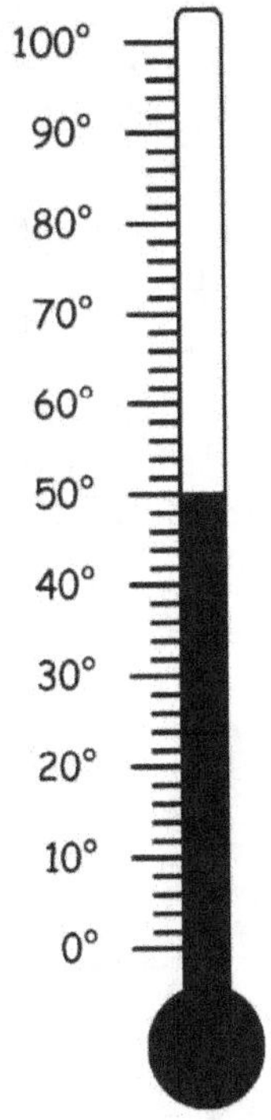

100° 90° 80° 70° 60° 50° 40° 30° 20° 10° 0°	100° 90° 80° 70° 60° 50° 40° 30° 20° 10° 0°
100° 90° 80° 70° 60° 50° 40° 30° 20° 10° 0°	100° 90° 80° 70° 60° 50° 40° 30° 20° 10° 0°

MEASURING TEMPERATURE

Directions: Write the correct temperature in each box.

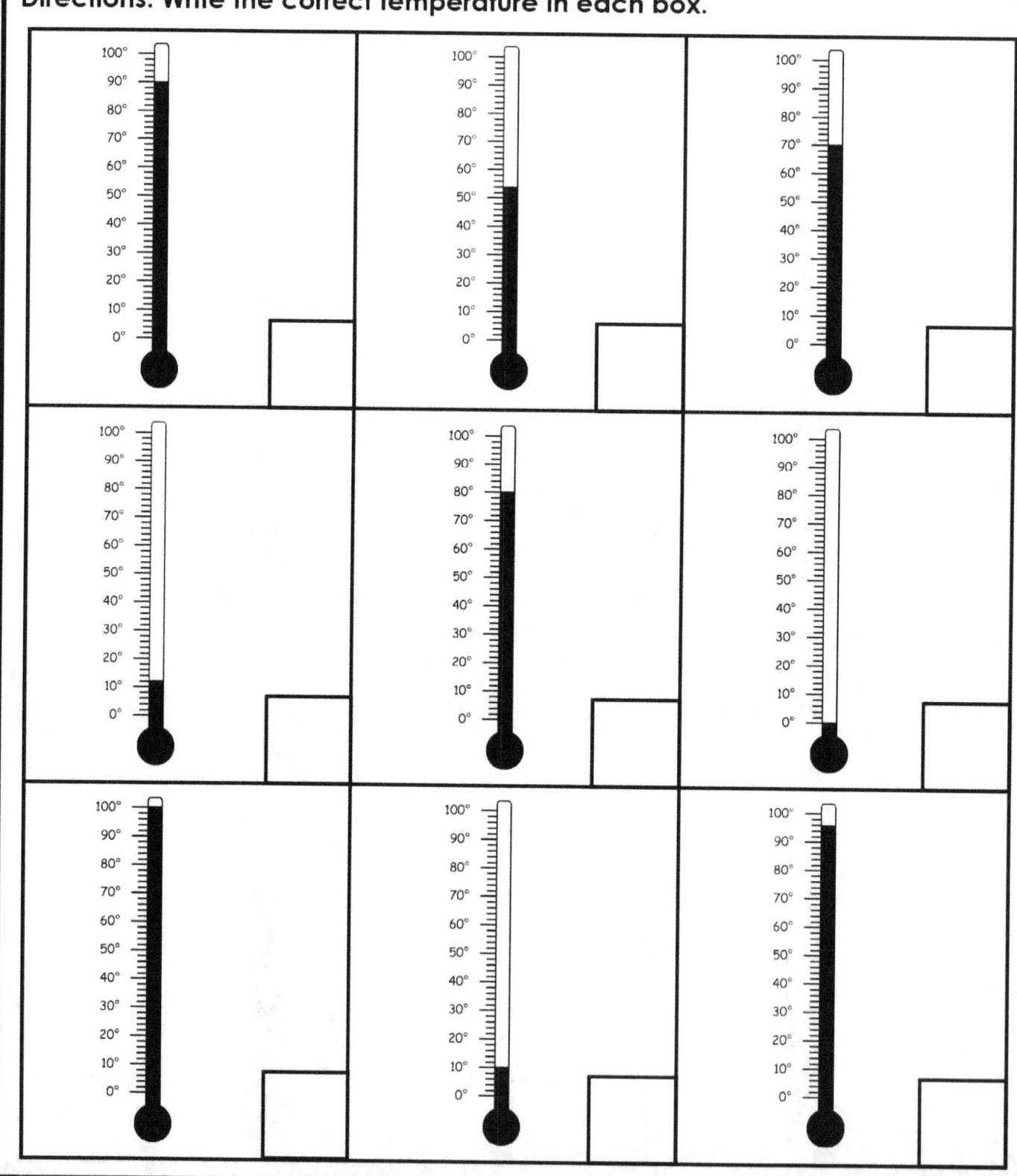

MEASURING TEMPERATURE

Directions: Draw a line between thermometers with same temperature.

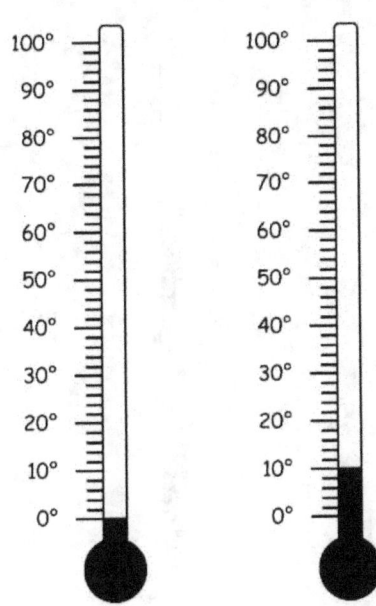
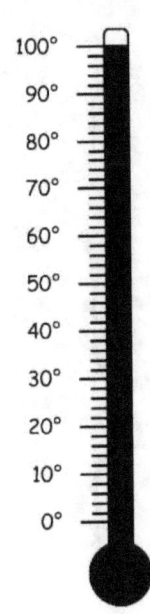
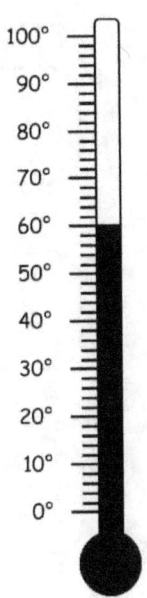
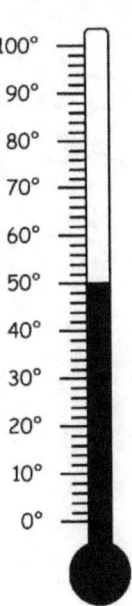
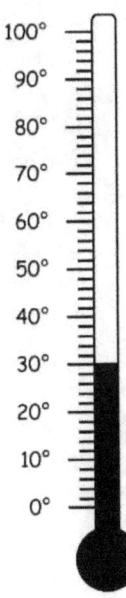

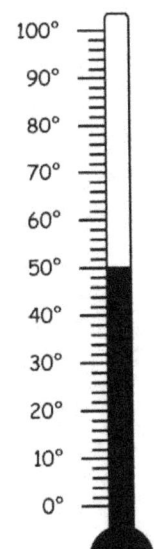
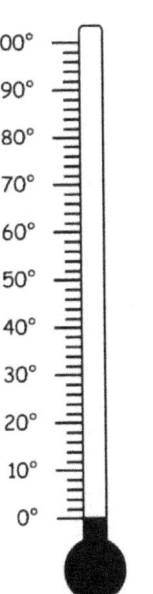
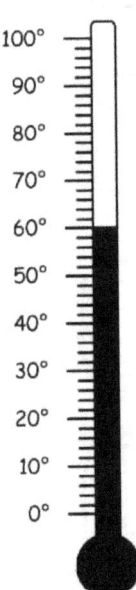
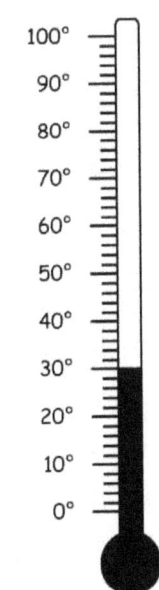
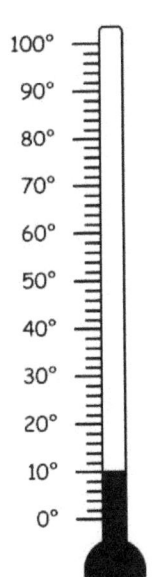
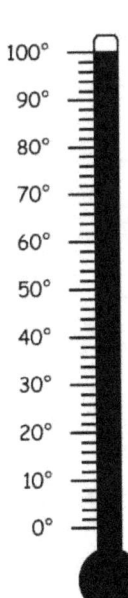

MEASURING TEMPERATURE

Directions: Draw a line from the scale to correct temperature.

50°

0 °

30°

78°

100°

90°

26°

62°

MEASURING TEMPERATURE

Directions: Color the thermometer with the correct temperature.

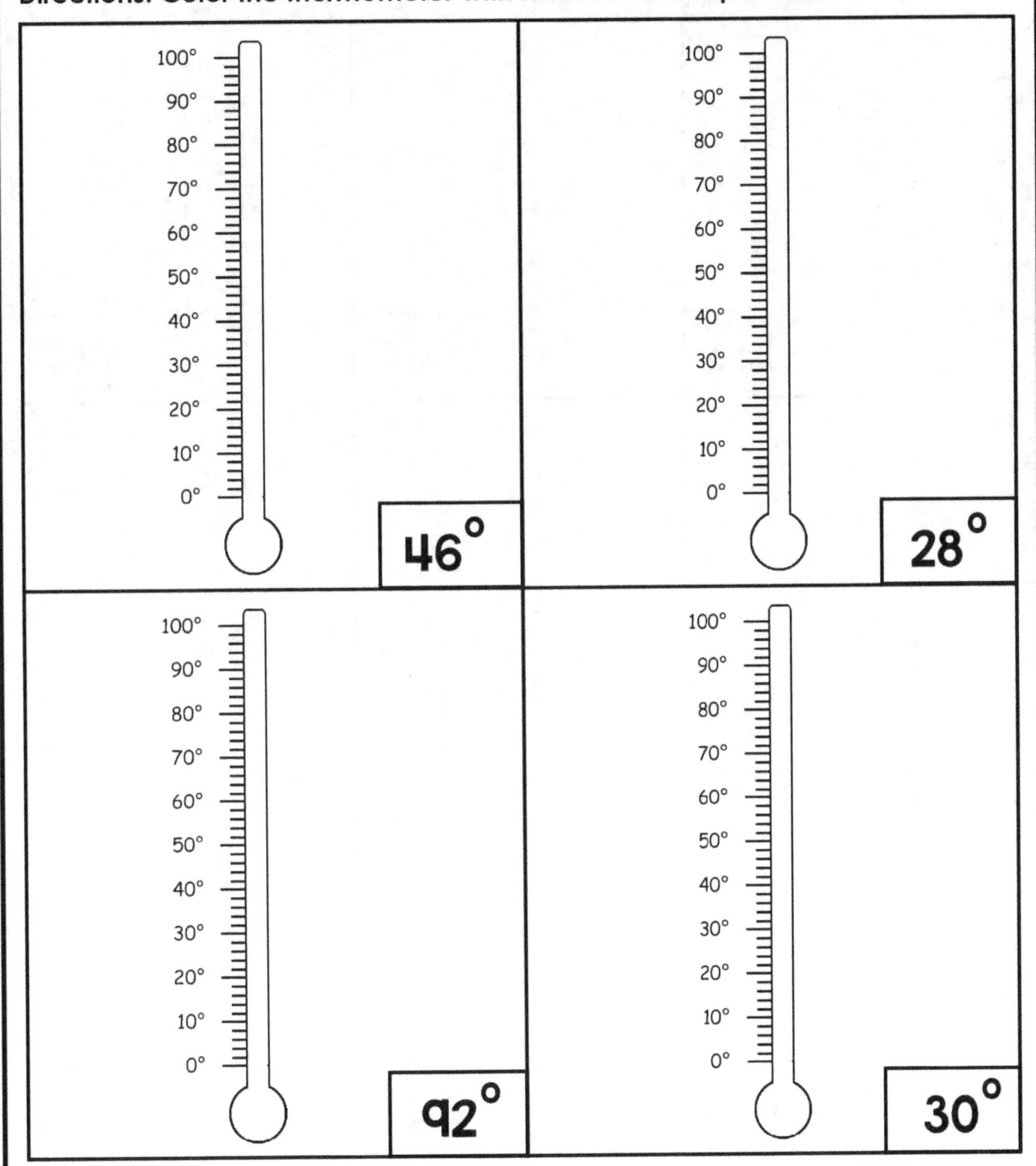

MEASURING TEMPERATURE

Directions: Color the thermometer with the correct temperature.

100° 90° 80° 70° 60° 50° 40° 30° 20° 10° 0° **18**	100° 90° 80° 70° 60° 50° 40° 30° 20° 10° 0° **30**	100° 90° 80° 70° 60° 50° 40° 30° 20° 10° 0° **10**
100° 90° 80° 70° 60° 50° 40° 30° 20° 10° 0° **62**	100° 90° 80° 70° 60° 50° 40° 30° 20° 10° 0° **70**	100° 90° 80° 70° 60° 50° 40° 30° 20° 10° 0° **86**
100° 90° 80° 70° 60° 50° 40° 30° 20° 10° 0° **38**	100° 90° 80° 70° 60° 50° 40° 30° 20° 10° 0° **44**	100° 90° 80° 70° 60° 50° 40° 30° 20° 10° 0° **100**

READING SCALE

Directions: Fill the blank with correct weight.

  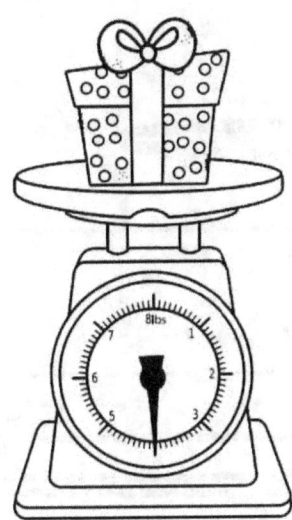 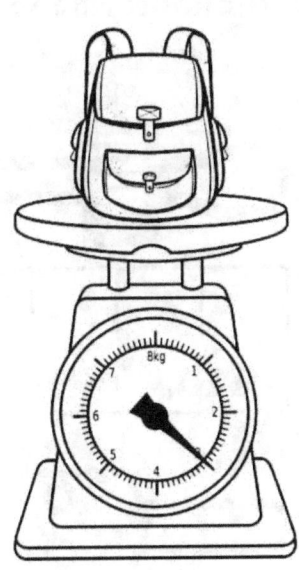

_____ lbs   _____ kg   _____ lbs   _____ kg

Directions: Fill the blank with correct temperature.

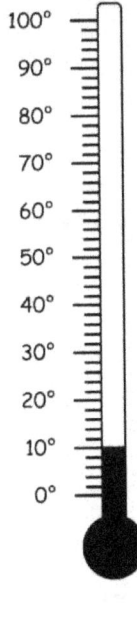 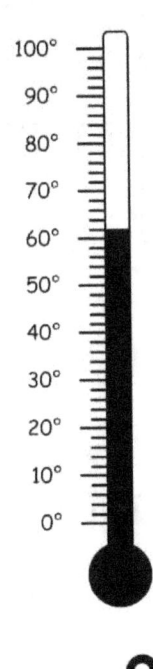 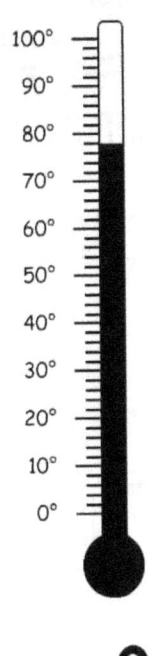 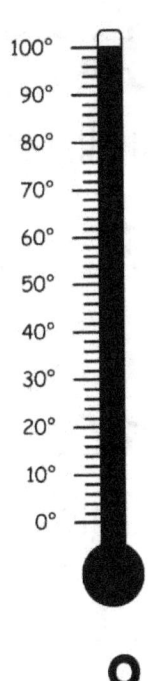

_____ °   _____ °   _____ °   _____ °

READING SCALE

Directions: Fill the blank with correct length.

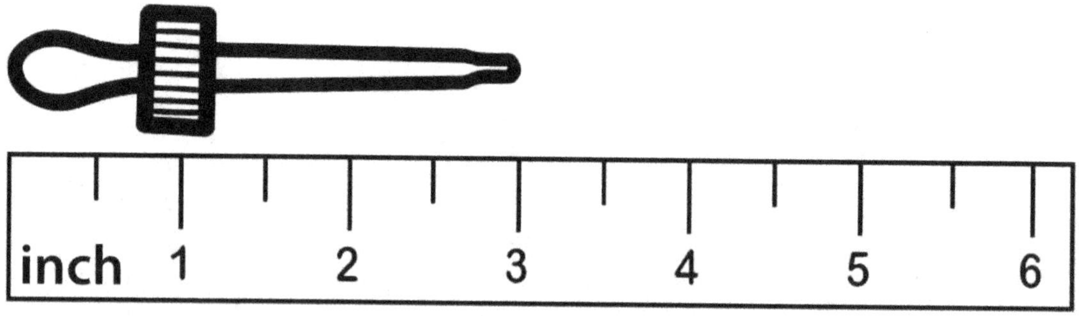

inch 1 2 3 4 5 6 ____ in

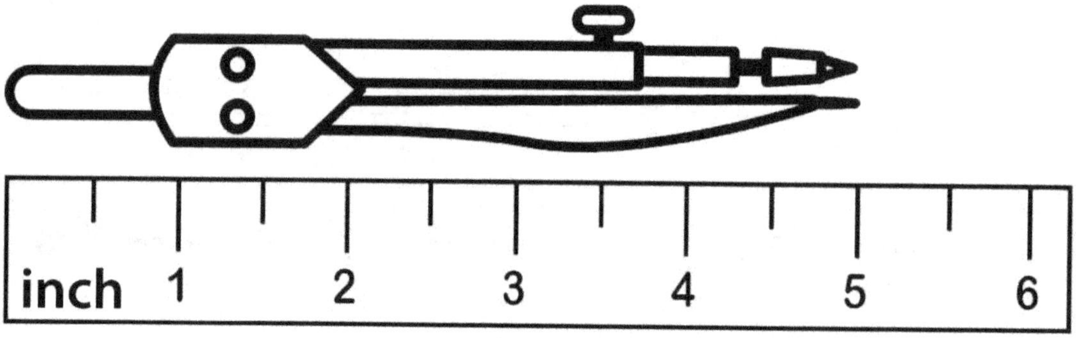

inch 1 2 3 4 5 6 ____ in

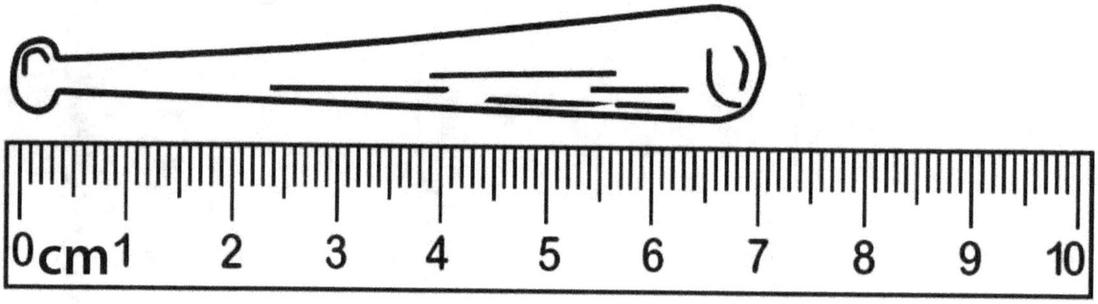

0cm1 2 3 4 5 6 7 8 9 10 ____ cm

0cm1 2 3 4 5 6 7 8 9 10 ____ cm

READING SCALE

Directions: Fill the blank with correct volume.

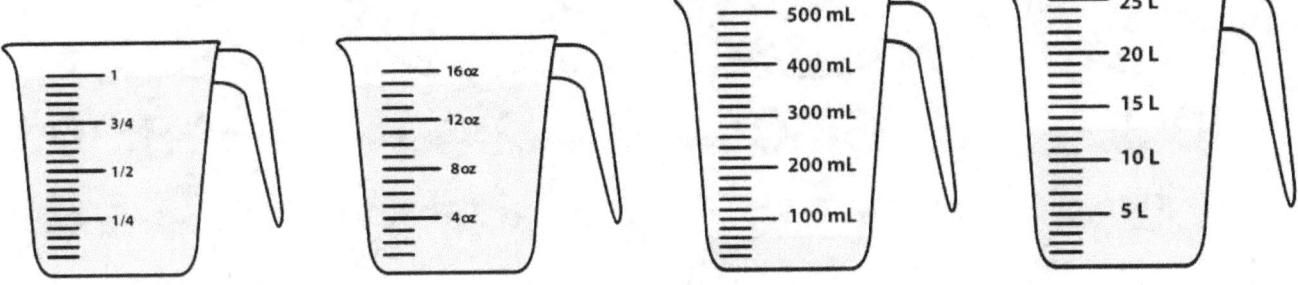

____ cup   ____ oz   ____ mL   ____ L

Directions: Fill the blank with correct weight.

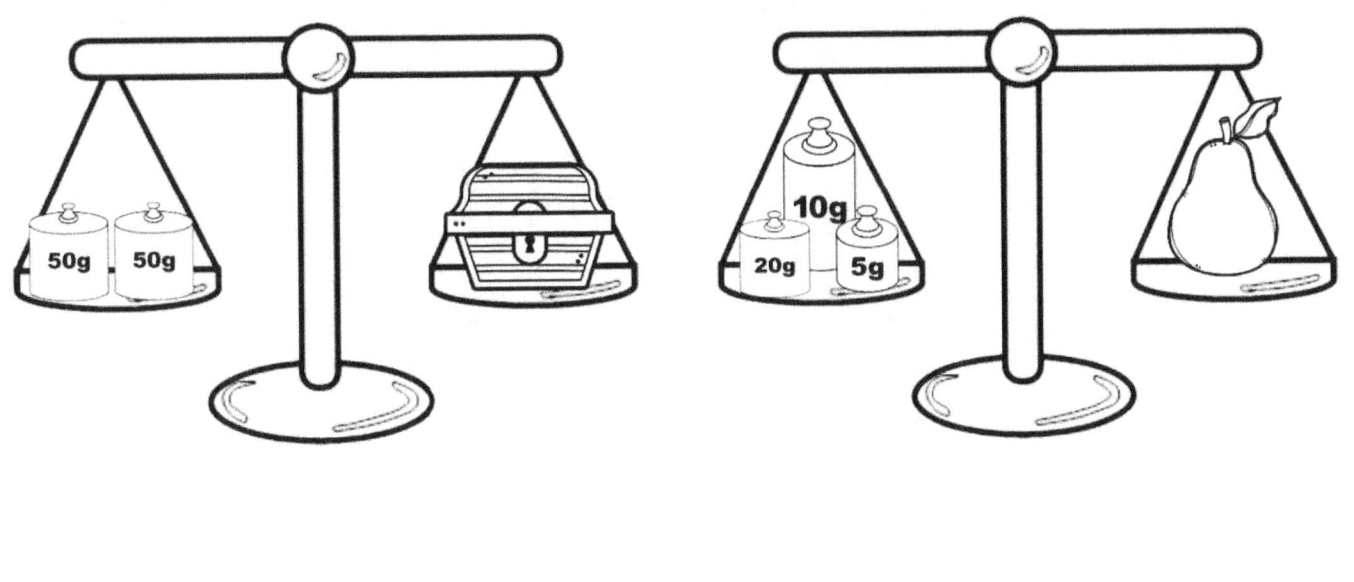

____ g   ____ g

READING SCALE

Directions: Draw hands on the clock face to show the time.

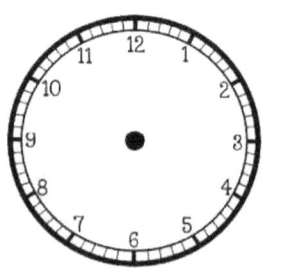 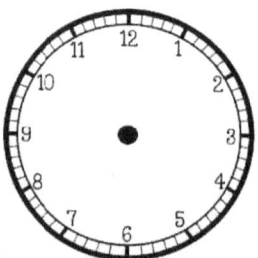 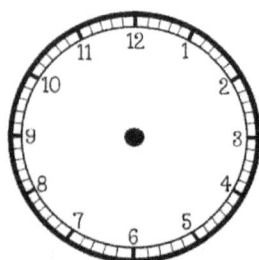 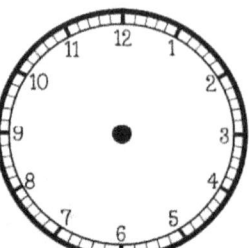

| 10:30 | 5:30 | 2:00 | 8:30 |

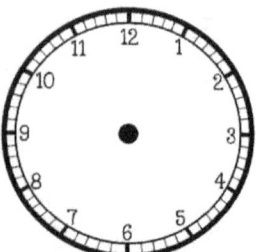 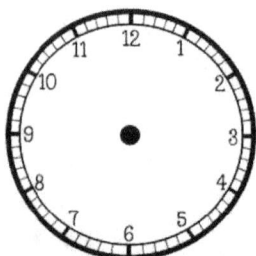 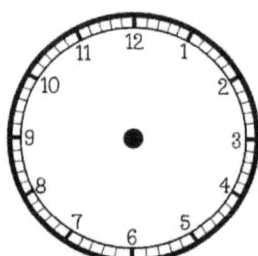 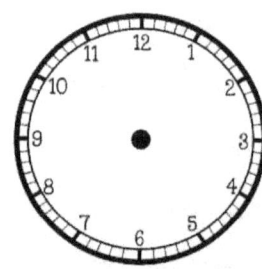

| 10:30 | 5:30 | 2:00 | 8:30 |

Directions: Color the thermometer with the correct temperature.

| 46° | 68° | 10° | 92° |

MEASURING LENGTH

Directions: Find each of these items in your home. Estimate the length of each item in inches. Then use your ruler to measure the actual lengths.

Item	Estimate	Actual Length

READING SCALE

Directions: Color the measuring cup to the correct volume.

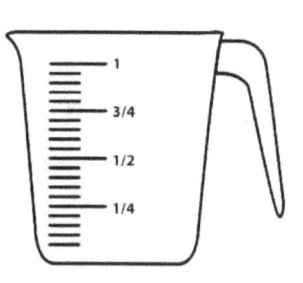 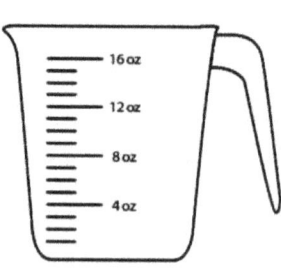 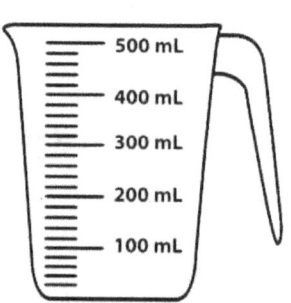 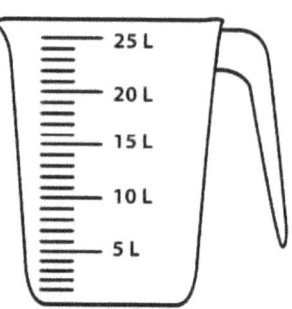

3/4 cup	14 oz	220 mL	8 L

 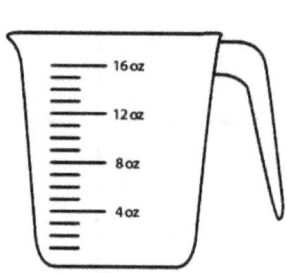 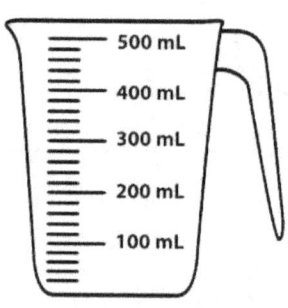 

1/2 cup	4 oz	80 mL	17 L

Directions: Color the ruler to the correct centimeters.

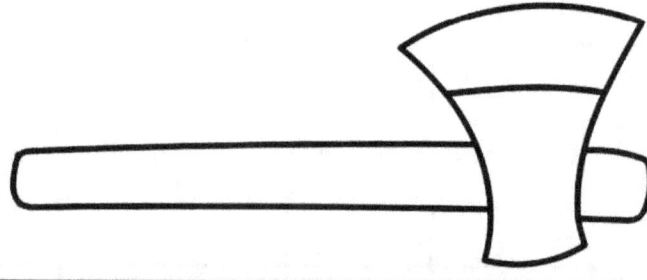

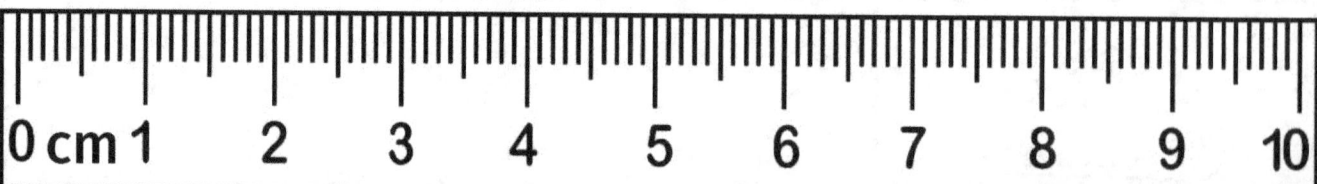

MEASURING LENGTH

Directions: Find these items in your home. Use your ruler and measure each item. Write your answer in box.

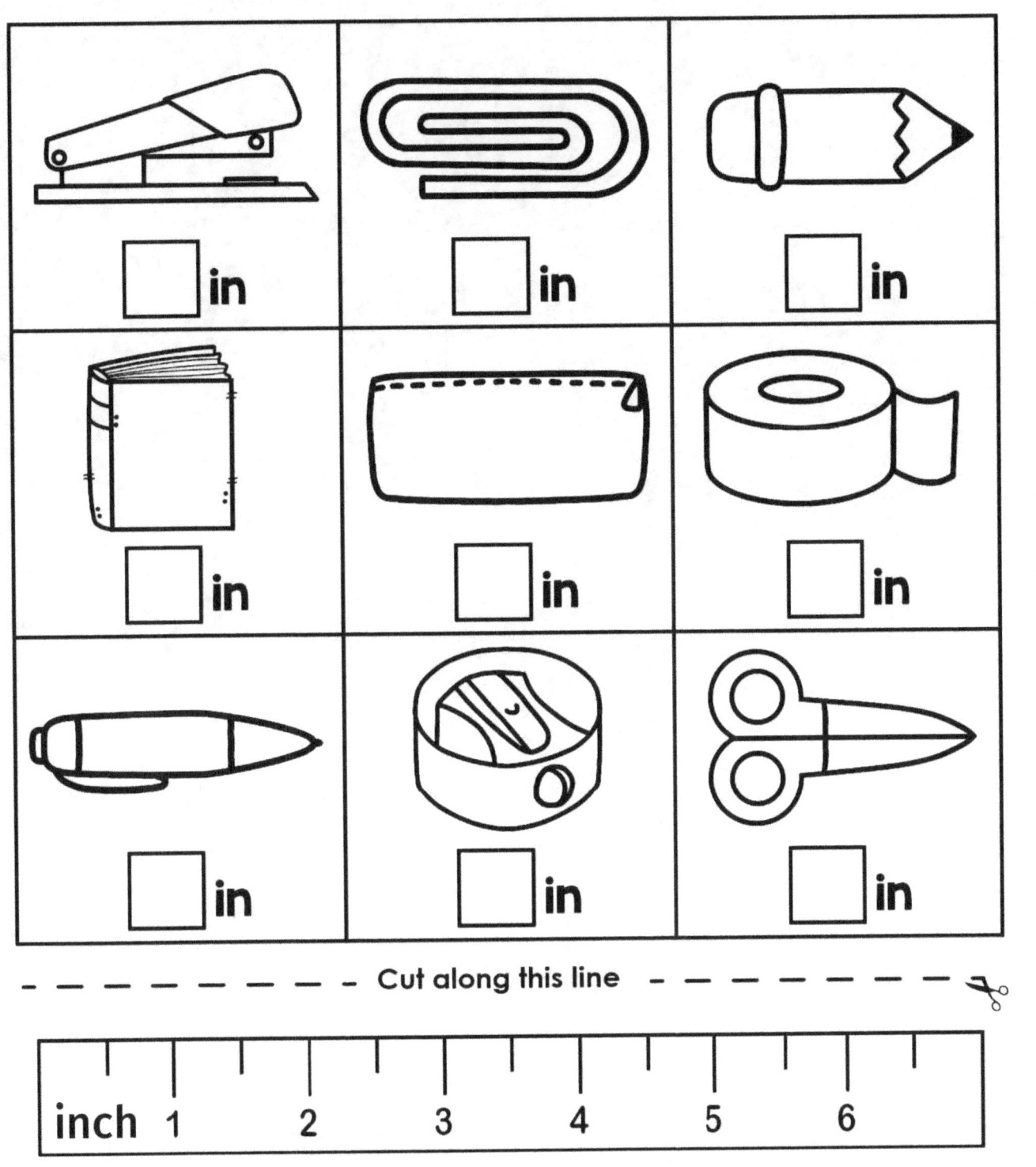

☐ in   ☐ in   ☐ in

☐ in   ☐ in   ☐ in

☐ in   ☐ in   ☐ in

- - - - - - - - - - - - - - Cut along this line - - - - - - - - - - - - - ✂

| inch | 1 | 2 | 3 | 4 | 5 | 6 |

MEASURING LENGTH

Directions: Use your ruler and measure the length of following items, and write your answer in the box.

◻ in

◻ in

◻ in

◻ in

◻ in

- - - - - - - - - Cut along this line - - - - - - - - - ✂

| inch | 1 | 2 | 3 | 4 | 5 | 6 |

MEASURING LENGTH

Directions: Use your ruler and measure the length of following items, and write your answer in the box.

[ ] in

[ ] in

[ ] in

[ ] in

[ ] in

- - - - - - - - - - Cut along this line - - - - - - - - - ✂

| inch | 1 | 2 | 3 | 4 | 5 | 6 |

MEASURING LENGTH

Directions: Use your ruler and measure either height OR width. Write your answer in the box.

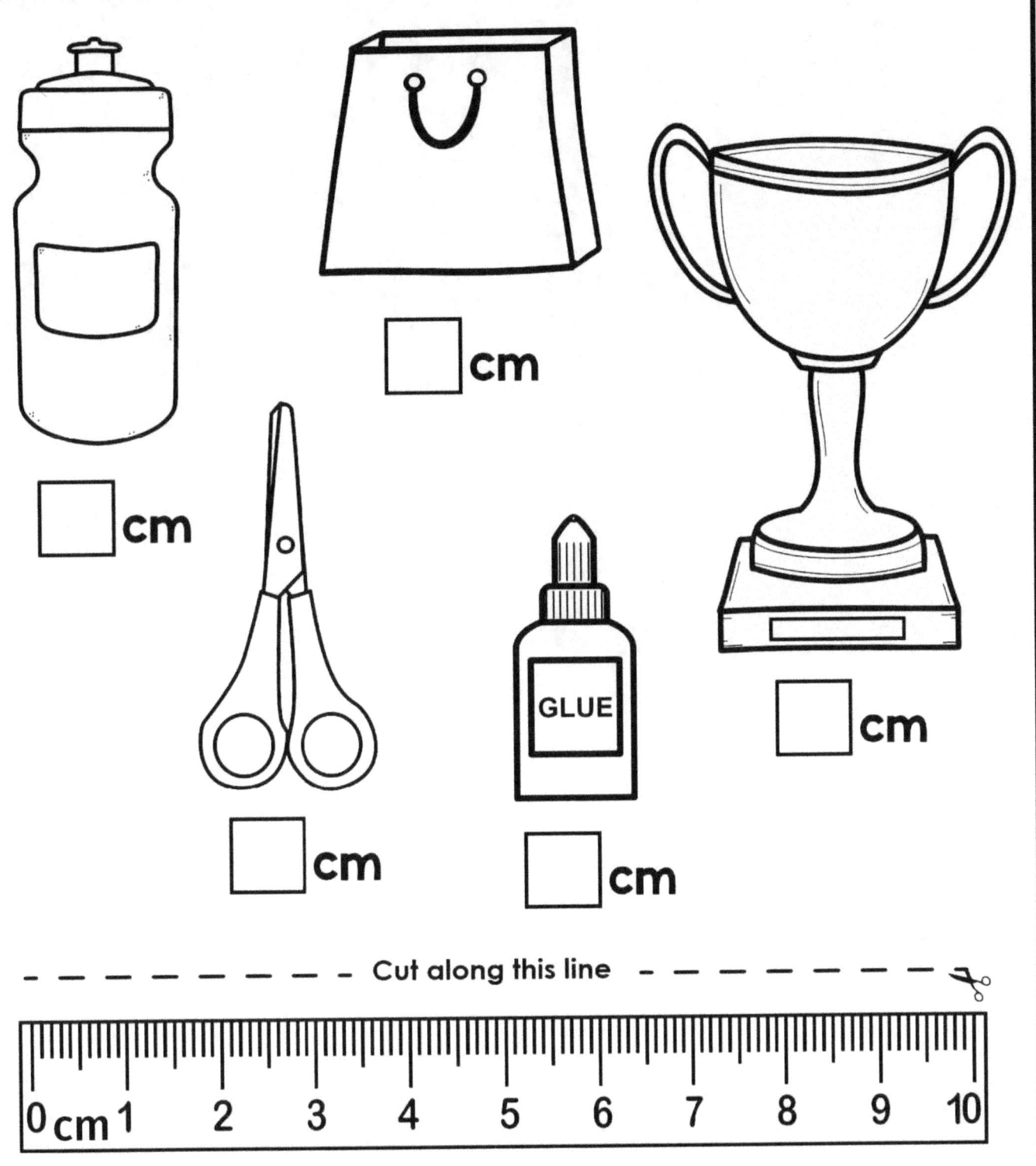

☐ cm

☐ cm

☐ cm

☐ cm

☐ cm

- - - - - - - - - Cut along this line - - - - - - - - - ✂

0 cm 1   2   3   4   5   6   7   8   9   10

MEASURING HEIGHT

Directions: Use your ruler and measure the height of following items, and write your answer in the box.

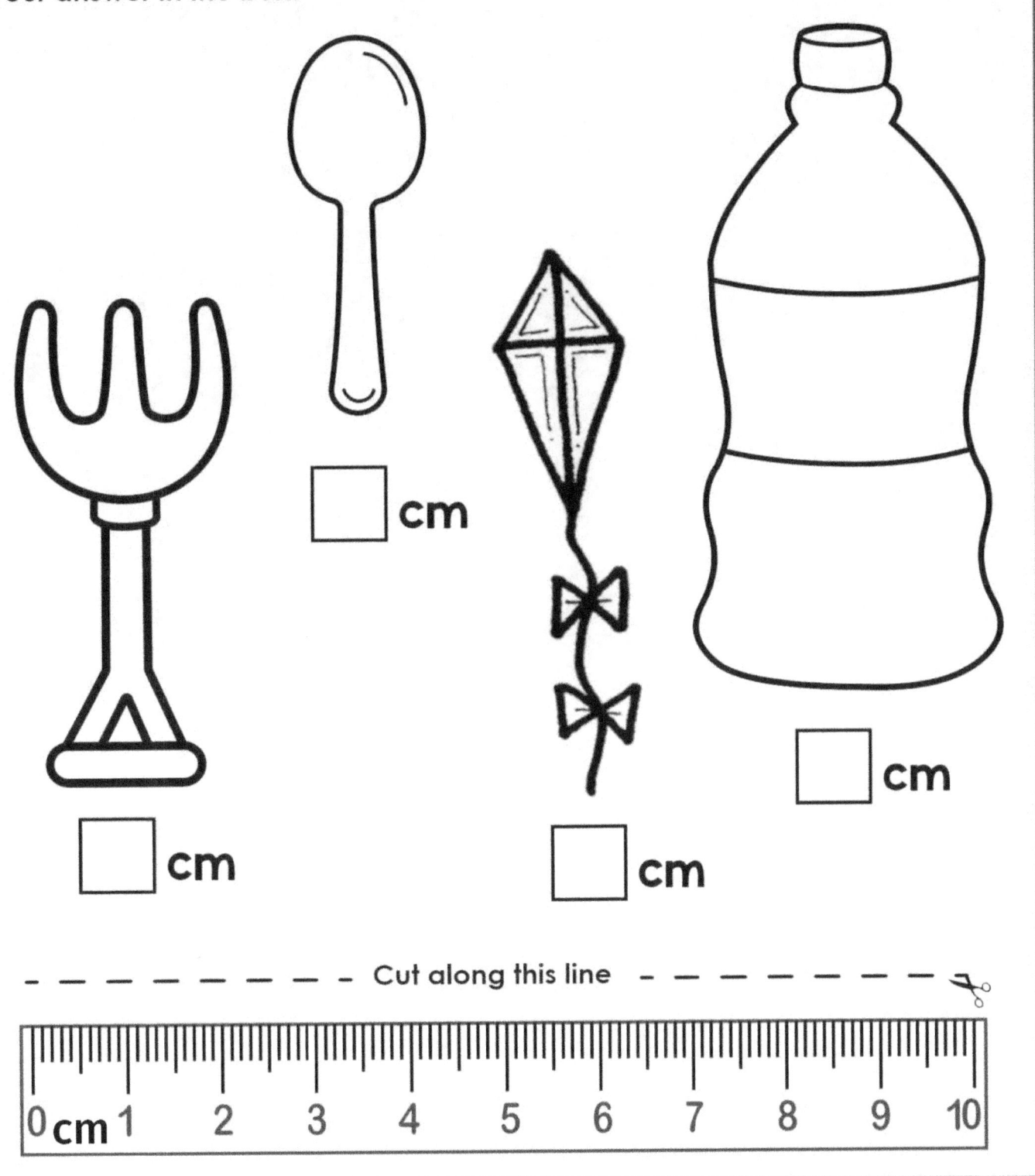

MEASURING LENGTH

Directions: Cut out the picture and paste them from tallest to shortest.

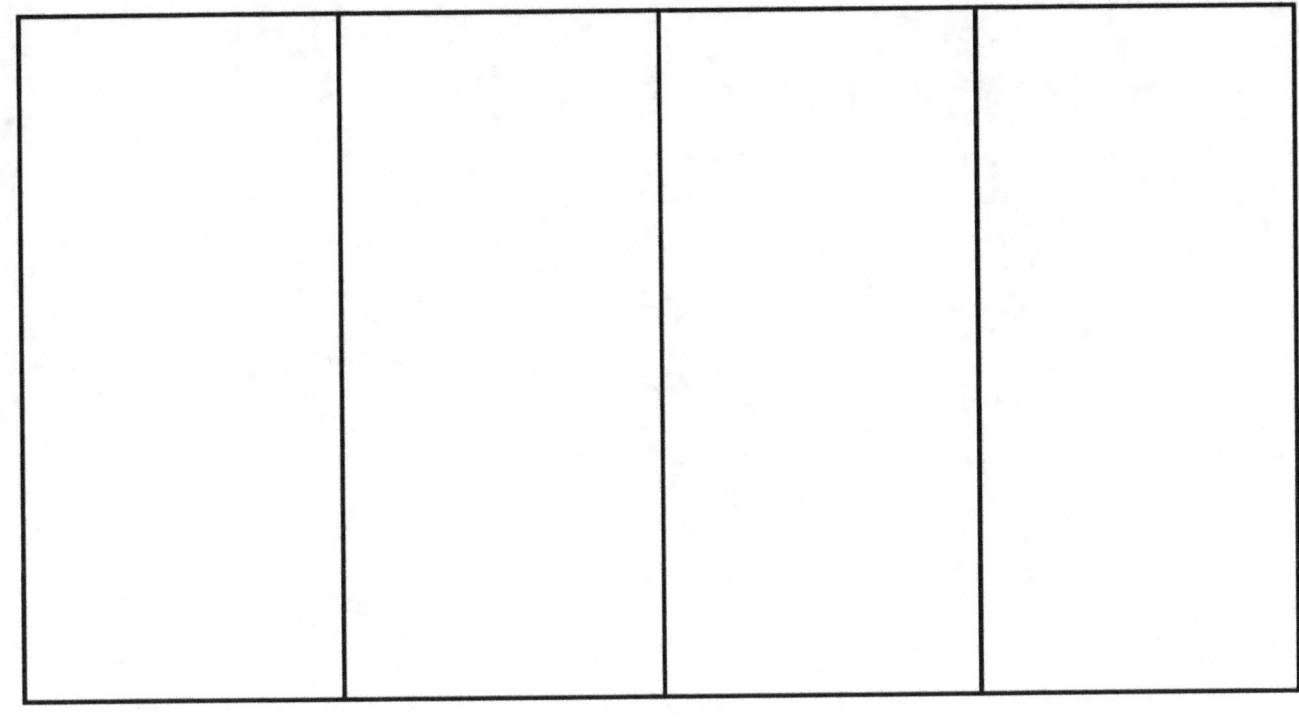

MEASURING WIDTH

Directions: Cut out the picture and arrange them according to their width.

Wide	Narrow

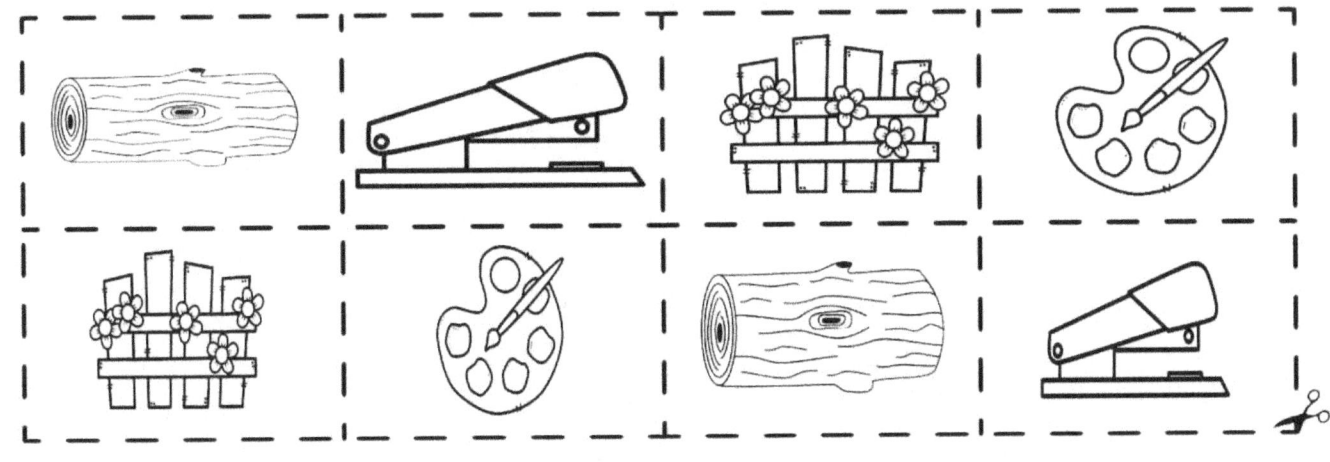

TELLING TIME

Directions: Cut out the time and paste them under the correct clock.

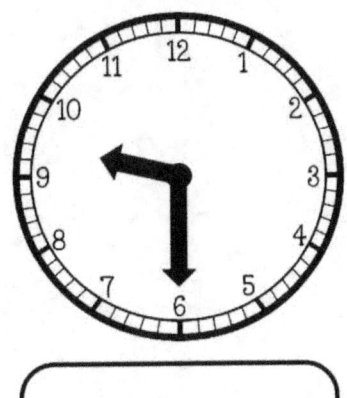

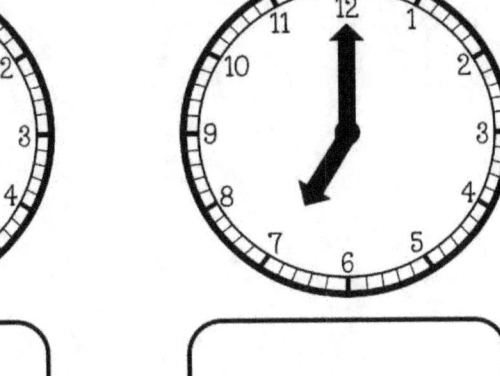

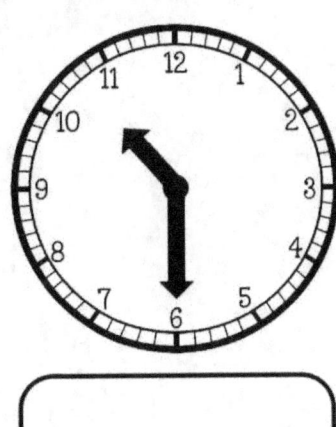

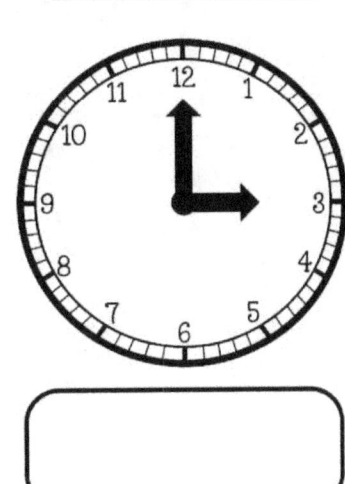

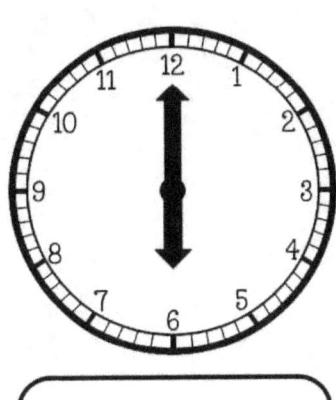

10:30	6:00	5:00
7:00	9:30	3:00

MEASURING VOLUME

Directions: Cut out the volume and paste them under correct measuring cup.

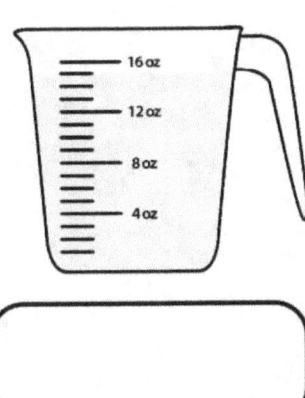

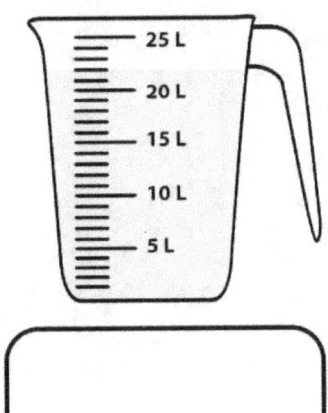

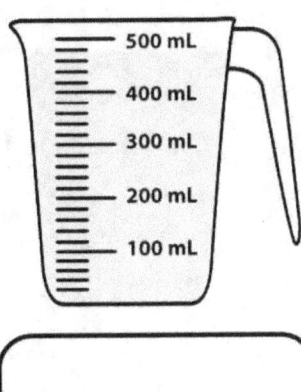

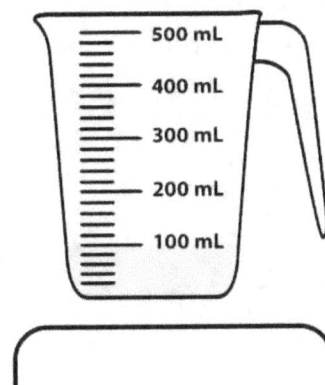

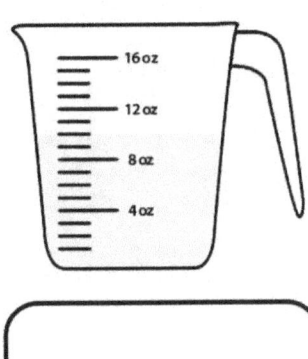

15 oz

480 mL

9 L

100 mL

22 L

10 oz

MEASURING TEMPERATURE

Directions: Cut out the picture and paste them on matching temperature.

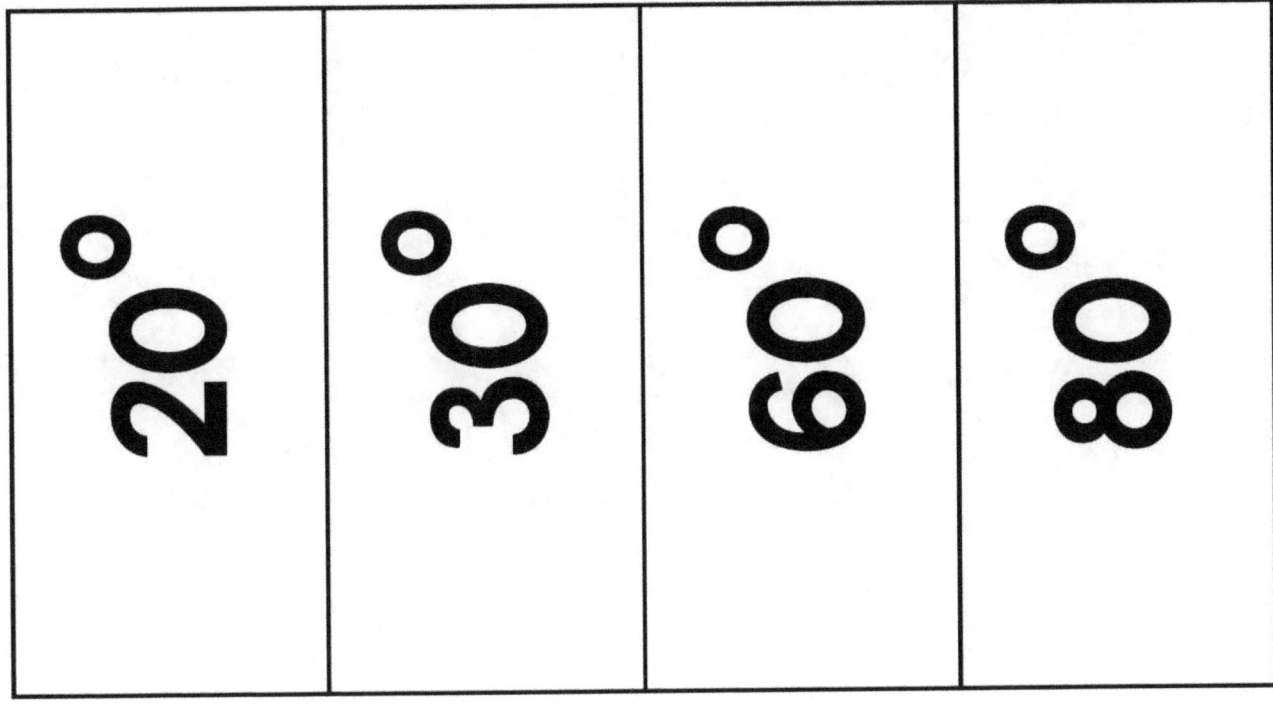

| 20° | 30° | 60° | 80° |

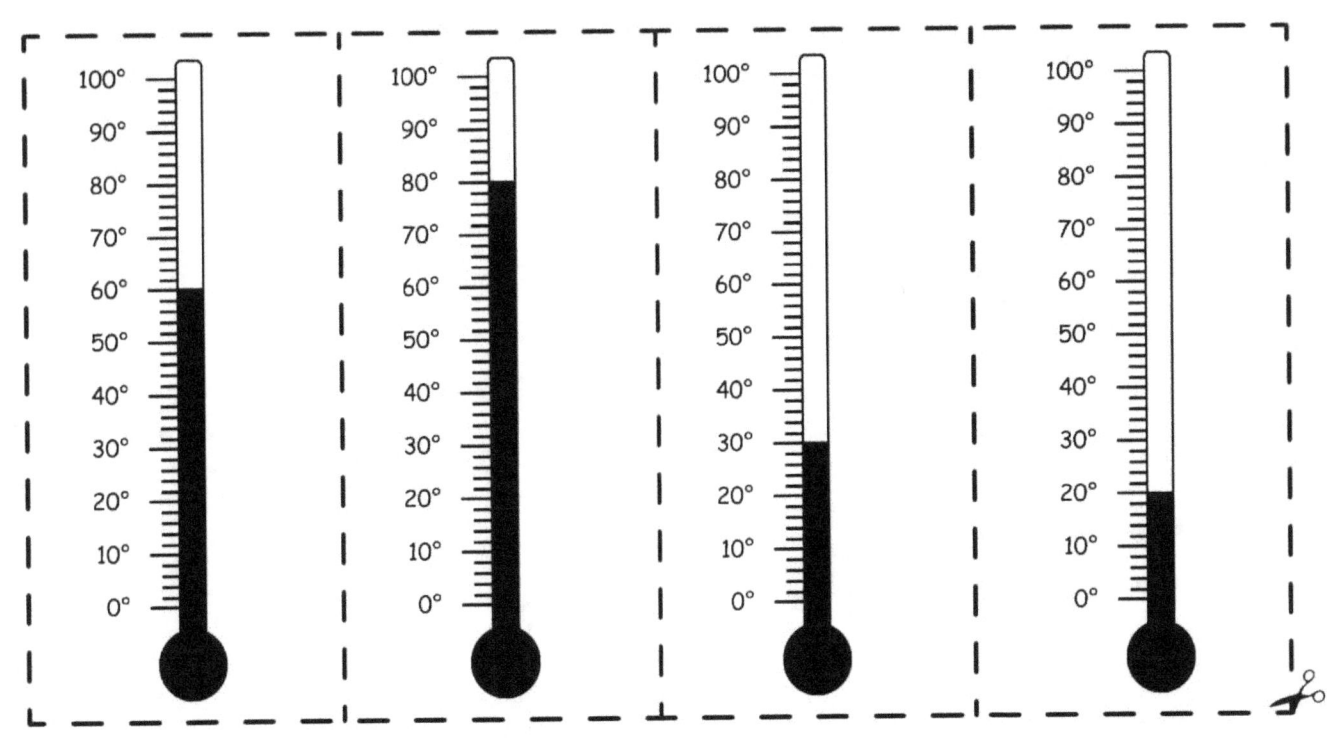

www.ingramcontent.com/pod-product-compliance
Lightning Source LLC
Chambersburg PA
CBHW080848120626
46553CB00009B/2622